WITHOUT RESERVATIONS

For my wife and family

and

Every Marriott associate, past and present, all over the world

 Luxury Custom Publishing, LLC
3920 Conde Street
San Diego, CA 92110

First edition December 2012

10 9 8 7 6 5 4 3 2 1

Printed in the United States of America

ISBN 978-0-9833-0333-6 (hardcover)
ISBN 978-0-9833-0334-3 (paperback)
ISBN 978-1-938120-74-9 (eBook)

Don't listen to what they say. Go see.

— CHINESE PROVERB

WITHOUT RESERVATIONS

HOW A FAMILY ROOT BEER STAND GREW INTO
A GLOBAL HOTEL COMPANY

Bill Marriott

J. W. MARRIOTT, JR.
AND KATHI ANN BROWN

LUXURY CUSTOM PUBLISHING · SAN DIEGO

CONTENTS

PART III: EMBRACE CHANGE

PART IV: ACT WITH INTEGRITY

PART V: SERVE OUR WORLD

AFTERWORD   156

"The world is a book; those who do not travel read only one page."

— SAINT AUGUSTINE

INTRODUCTION

*"Nothing great in the world
has been accomplished without passion."*

— G. W. F. HEGEL, philosopher

For 60 years, I have loved my job, without reservations. While many people my age look forward to their daily round of golf or a dip in the pool, I prefer to travel halfway around the world to inspect hotels.

My youngest son, David, now chief operations officer for our eastern region hotels in the Americas, loves to tell a story about the time his grade school teacher asked the class to draw pictures of their fathers at work and at play. Without a second thought, David sketched two images: In one, I'm wearing a suit and tie, seated at a large desk with a pen in my hand. In the other, I'm dressed in a sweater, seated at a smaller desk with a pen in my hand.

I'm not proud of all the hours I spent away from my family during my career, but I am proud that my passion for the work I do inspired all four of my children to follow me into the hotel business. Like me, they each treasure the special culture that has always made Marriott International a great place to work.

An organization's culture is not a small matter. A few years ago, a group of business students at Brigham Young University (BYU) decided to study the impact of corporate culture on a business's bottom line. They focused on three major players in the hospitality industry: Starwood, Hilton and Marriott.

After months of in-depth research and analysis, the students released their findings. Their main takeaway? Culture counts. In Marriott's case, our culture results in measurably lower employee turnover and higher customer satisfaction, a winning combination that boosts our profits and pleases our shareholders.

I wasn't surprised by the BYU study's conclusion. Marriott's corporate culture is the keystone of our global operations and has been ever since my parents, J. Willard and Alice Sheets Marriott, opened a tiny A&W root beer stand on 14th Street NW in Washington, D.C., in May 1927. Today, more than eight decades later, the same basic principles that helped to launch our company are still in place, still fueling Marriott's growth and still differentiating us from our peers in an increasingly competitive global hotel marketplace.

What are those fundamental principles — or what we call our core values?

They're five brief, powerful aspirations that are easy to remember but challenging to live up to:

Put people first.

Pursue excellence.

Embrace change.

Act with integrity.

Serve our world.

The first item of the five has been our company credo since my parents' era. "Take care of your employees, and they'll take care of your customers" was the daily mantra that my brother, Dick, and I heard from our father while we were growing up. Marriott still draws its strength today from our deep belief that treating

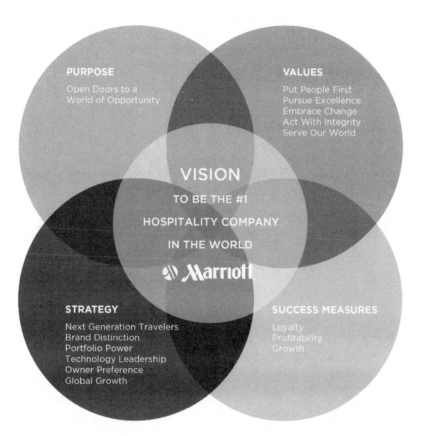

PURPOSE
Open Doors to a
World of Opportunity

VALUES
Put People First
Pursue Excellence
Embrace Change
Act With Integrity
Serve Our World

VISION
TO BE THE #1
HOSPITALITY COMPANY
IN THE WORLD
Marriott.

STRATEGY
Next Generation Travelers
Brand Distinction
Portfolio Power
Technology Leadership
Owner Preference
Global Growth

SUCCESS MEASURES
Loyalty
Profitability
Growth

PURPOSE

We Open Doors to a World of Opportunity for our:

PEOPLE
Personal and professional growth

CUSTOMERS
Rewarding travel experiences

OWNERS & FRANCHISEES
Profitable investments

INVESTORS
Financial achievement

BUSINESS ALLIANCES
Collaboration with suppliers and other key relationships

COMMUNITIES
A more sustainable future in the places where we live and work

VALUES

Our enduring core values set us apart from the competition:

PUT PEOPLE FIRST
Take care of associates and they will take care of the customers

PURSUE EXCELLENCE
Dedication to the customer through service excellence

EMBRACE CHANGE
Success is never final

ACT WITH INTEGRITY
How we do business is as important as the business we do

SERVE OUR WORLD
Our "spirit to serve℠" makes our culture more vibrant, our business stronger, and the world a better place

STRATEGY

We have a six-part strategy:

NEXT GENERATION TRAVELERS
Understand and attract Gen X, Y and future guests

BRAND DISTINCTION
Invest in innovation and differentiation

PORTFOLIO POWER
Build loyalty with the most compelling family of brands

TECHNOLOGY LEADERSHIP
Empower connections for guests and associates

OWNER PREFERENCE
Generate value for our hotel owners and franchisees

GLOBAL GROWTH
Expand our footprint and profitability

SUCCESS MEASURES

Our vision is to be the #1 hospitality company in the world, leading on three success measures:

LOYALTY

PROFITABILITY

GROWTH

Marriott International's Core Values are connected to our Vision, Purpose, Strategy and Success Measures our associates — our word for employees — with the respect they deserve helps them do a phenomenal job for our guests.

The other four values likewise stretch back in time to the earliest days of the company, 30 years before we ever thought about building our first hotel. Our popular Hot Shoppes restaurants were the low-tech Facebook of their day — casual gathering places where families, neighbors, kids and cops caught up on the day's news, shared jokes, flirted, celebrated birthdays and just hung out. Customers could count on spotless dishes and shiny floors ("Pursue excellence"), an ever-growing menu ("Embrace change"), honest value for their money ("Act with integrity") and a true sense of community second to none ("Serve our world"). My picky father wouldn't have had it any other way.

Marriott has come a long, long way from the days of being known as a regional family restaurant chain, but our values haven't budged an inch. In fact, they've deepened over time into a commitment to do what great companies should do: make a lasting, positive difference in the world. Successful companies like ours are about more than simply making money. We can empower individuals and help to build stable communities at a time when many of our traditional social institutions are struggling with shrinking budgets and growing demand for their services. Marriott's sense of social responsibility finds expression in myriad ways, from reducing our carbon footprint to preserving endangered natural areas to investing in education and other initiatives that will improve the quality of life for our associates, their families and their communities.

I'm particularly proud of the fact that Marriott creates opportunities. For our associates. Our hotel owners. Our investors. Our partners. Our guests. And for the hundreds of localities in which we operate around the world.

I remember when we opened our first hotel in Warsaw. The year was 1989. The Berlin Wall fell that November. At the time, we were the only Western hotel company managing a hotel in Eastern Europe. We also had the only reliable international telephone system in Poland. The hotel quickly became the place to go to conduct business. To fill our staff positions, we reached out to all sorts of people who had never worked in hotels. We brought them to the United States, trained them, and they returned to Poland to work as supervisors. We're doing something similar in Rwanda, where we're working with the Akilah Institute for Women, based in Kigali, to train 14 young women in hospitality management. In turn, they'll train as many as 250 of their countrymen to work at our hotels in Kigali. I love the fact that Marriott offers these kinds of life-changing opportunities every day, in dozens of countries around the world, and in the United States, too.

The founding of Marriott is itself a textbook example of a golden opportunity spotted and seized. My parents saw the chance to better their lives and went for it with gusto. My dad came through hot, sticky Washington, D.C., in late summer 1921 while heading home to Utah from his mission for the Mormon Church. At some point after getting back to Salt Lake City he noticed cars lined up for blocks at the local A&W root beer stand. Salt Lake City wasn't as hot as the nation's capital. A light bulb went on in his head. It took some doing, but my father persuaded A&W to sell him the first A&W root beer franchise east of the Mississippi.

Dad's itch to start a small business could not have been better timed. The recent invention of the automobile and airplane promised to revolutionize transportation. So many Americans took to the roads and skies in the first half of the 20th century that the era was nicknamed the Golden Age of Travel.

My parents were among those on the move. On their wedding day in early 1927, they jumped into a Model T Ford and headed to Washington, D.C., from Salt Lake City. With only a bit of cash lent to them by my grandmother from her cookie jar, they bounced along the nation's rough dirt roads for 11 days to reach their destination. On rainy days, the roads turned to mud and the Ford would slide into a ditch. The pair would walk to the nearest town and find someone willing to pull them out.

When the couple finally reached Washington, they moved into an apartment with some friends and got busy on the root beer franchise. When the weather turned cold, my mother cooked up the idea of adding hot food like tamales and chili to the menu. They called their restaurant the Hot Shoppes. A year later, they opened the first drive-in east of the Mississippi River. From there the business grew like crazy, even during the Great Depression.

My parents' honeymoon trip across the country wasn't glamorous, but it certainly was memorable. More than 85 years later, Marriott's main business is to help new generations of people create their own travel experiences. Travel — particularly world travel — opens minds, broadens horizons, erases borders and helps us all appreciate and celebrate, instead of fear, our differences.

Following the terrorist attacks of September 11, 2001, travel lost some of its allure for many people. The public's trepidation was understandable, but to my mind, getting out to see and to experience our world became more important than ever. At a time when tensions can rise to a fever pitch almost overnight, the more of us who travel, the better. With every trip, we chip away at the barriers that give rise to misunderstanding, fear and violence.

Fortunately, in spite of troubling hot spots of unrest around the world, all signs are pointing toward the dawn of a new Golden Age of Travel. In 2012, for the first time, as many as 1 billion people — that's right, 1 billion people — are expected to travel outside their own countries. What an amazing figure. And an amazing opportunity for adventure seekers and for those of us who believe in the power of travel to change the world.

One of the most striking worldwide trends of the past 50 years or so has been the expansion of the middle class. Hundreds of millions of people have enough money, freedom and curiosity to travel outside their home countries for the first time. China is probably the most dramatic example. Not very long ago, travel into and out of the country was a mere trickle. But the explosion of economic growth there in the past 15 to 20 years has opened the floodgates to travel to and from China unlike anything I expected to see in my lifetime.

Naturally, Marriott plans to play a major role in promoting this new era of international exploration. Our ambition is nothing short of becoming the number one hospitality company in the world.

Thanks to the flood of global adventurers, the world's travel industry expects to create several million jobs in 2012 alone. And that's why I've worked tirelessly to make sure government and business work together to welcome the world's new travelers. In the United States, that means expedited visa processes and friendly customs and entry experiences.

While Marriott is busy working toward that lofty goal, my own role at Marriott is changing. I turned 80 in March 2012. I don't think anyone should be CEO of a major business at that age. So I handed off the role to Arne Sorenson on March 31. But I'm still executive chairman. And I don't plan to go anywhere any time soon. After spending better than 60 years in the company I wouldn't know what to do with myself if I didn't have an office to go to. Besides, Donna, my lovely wife of 57 years, says she married me "for better and for worse … but not for lunch."

PART I:
PUT PEOPLE FIRST

"Take care of your employees,
and they'll take care of your customers."

— J. WILLARD MARRIOTT
co-founder (with Alice Sheets Marriott), Hot Shoppes

CHAPTER 1:
PAY IT FORWARD

CHAPTER 2:
HE WHO LISTENS WELL
LEARNS MORE

CHAPTER 3:
ALL FOR ONE,
ONE FOR ALL

1

PAY IT FORWARD

"Remember, the deepest principle of human nature
is the craving to be appreciated."

— WILLIAM JAMES, psychologist

On March 25, 2012, I checked into the JW Marriott® Los Angeles L.A. LIVE. I had put a lot of sweat equity into getting this hotel complex open and operating under our flagship Marriott Hotels & Resorts® and The Ritz-Carlton® brands. Multiple meetings with the powerful ownership group AEG helped clinch the deal. I had attended ground breakings and grand openings with then California Governor Arnold Schwarzenegger and L.A. Mayor Antonio Villaraigosa, both of whom were committed to revitalizing downtown Los Angeles. The hotel is one of our most spectacular.

I settled into my room and got ready to meet with 1,300 of Marriott's top leaders, some of whom had flown halfway around the globe to be there. This would be our first Global General Managers meeting in five years. Since our last meeting in San Francisco, there had been a global economic crisis, widespread political upheaval across the Middle East and North Africa and I had announced that I would be relinquishing the CEO role at Marriott after 40 years in the job.

The giant ballroom where we were gathered was decked out with massive wide-screen monitors and a large stage that allowed the audience to envelop the guest speakers, which included Starbucks CEO Howard Schultz.

When it was my turn to speak, I was introduced by my handpicked successor, our new CEO, Arne Sorenson. The room reverberated with applause, and everyone stood up as I hustled up to the stage. Looking out into the sea of faces around me, I realized that I could name nearly every person in that room. I had visited their hotels, walked the loading docks and toured the kitchens, quizzed them on their occupancy rates and counted on them to deliver results for our company. Together we had weathered recessions, worried about budgets, hatched big plans and built gorgeous hotels all over the world. During hundreds of conversations, I had come to know them, their spouses, their children and very often their private hopes and struggles, too. I found myself tearing up more than once as I tried to convey a lifetime's worth of gratitude for their hard work and dedication to our company. The applause that followed was among the sweetest I've ever heard.

As I settled back into my chair, I thought about how much Marriott's success has rested in the hands of great associates like those who were seated around me. For more than eight decades, our company has been fortunate to attract and keep phenomenally talented people who easily could have chosen other paths, other companies, other opportunities.

My dad, J. Willard Marriott, deserves a lot of the credit for creating a culture that empowers our associates to give 110 percent day in, day out, year in, year out. A thoroughgoing extrovert, he loved to stroll through the company's restaurants and hotels greeting customers and employees. Dad particularly enjoyed spending time with the company's hourly associates. Marriott's corporate legend is full of stories of my father perched comfortably on a hotel lobby sofa, listening to the family problems of one of our associates while senior managers cooled their heels waiting for him to return to the office. Dad felt very strongly that the concerns and problems of the people who worked for him were always worth listening to. In his eyes, a successful company puts its employees first.

I couldn't agree more. When employees know that their problems will be taken seriously, that their ideas and insights matter, they're more comfortable and confident. In turn, they're better equipped to deliver their best on the job.

Everyone wins: the company, the employee, the customer.

The philosophy of putting our associates first is particularly important in our industry, because Marriott is in the people business. We don't manufacture any products. We're not a mail-order operation. Almost all of the 300,000 associates in our managed and franchised hotels interact with our guests, if only for a moment or two while passing in the corridor or seating them in the dining room.

What happens during those moments of interaction — what we call "touch points" — can make all the difference between a customer's satisfaction and disappointment. That's because even if our customers aren't always conscious of it, they have definite expectations about not only the tangible parts of eating and sleeping — good food, a comfortable bed — but also the intangibles of those experiences: how they're greeted, how their questions are answered, how their problems are handled. That's where the human touch determines whether an experience is poor, mediocre, positive or truly unforgettable.

No surprise, if the people who are responsible for supplying that human touch are unhappy, tired, stressed out, poorly trained, dissatisfied or otherwise distracted, they're going to have a tough time doing a good job. Their problems at home or behind the scenes will show in their work and have a direct impact on guests' experiences.

On the flip side, if our associates are content, confident and generally happy with themselves and the job, their positive attitude will be felt in everything they do. And if associates know that they're empowered to do whatever is needed to make a guest's stay top-notch, they'll do amazing things. We have countless associates who have demonstrated remarkable personal generosity and kindness toward guests over the years. If those associates didn't feel terrific about themselves, I don't think they would be able to do some of the things they've done. Some have loaned money out of their own pockets to guests who forgot their wallets. Others have played emergency babysitter, ordered (and picked up) replacement contact lenses, put their weekend mechanic skills to work on conked-out cars and mended well-loved stuffed animals in need of a few stitches.

Stories abound at Marriott about associates who don't hesitate when it comes to doing the right thing. When a few survivors of the now legendary emergency plane landing in New York City's Hudson River in January 2009 (headed by Captain "Sully" Sullenberger) showed up cold, wet and barefoot at the New York Marriott Marquis®, front desk associates snatched up petty cash and ran to a local sporting goods store to buy sweatpants, sweatshirts, socks and sneakers for them.

A laundry attendant at a Marriott hotel in Texas once spent two hours helping a guest who was in double arm casts do her hair and makeup, brush her teeth and tie her shoes so she could get out the door on time to see her son's championship soccer game. One of our hotel general managers went "dumpster diving" to retrieve a young guest's dental retainer. I laugh when I picture the GM, nattily attired in a suit and tie, skulking through the dumpster, determined to find the lost retainer.

I've heard dozens of stories about associates who've lent jewelry, coats, blouses and other items to guests who didn't pack them. One associate lent a nervous guest whose luggage was missing an entire suit for a critical job interview. Another simply gave a pair of her shoes outright to a guest when the guest discovered that she hadn't packed dress shoes for an important meeting.

When you have associates who are willing to give a guest the clothes off their backs, doesn't taking good care of those associates make sense? Yet in these economically challenged times, the idea of helping employees feel good about themselves seems to be absent from many companies' philosophies. To my mind, those companies are missing out on an opportunity to thank their employees for making their businesses successful.

I'm not about to claim that every Marriott associate has always been treated with unfailing fairness and unflagging support. No institution handles human problems perfectly every time. But I do think that we are well above average, thanks to the emphasis we place on the idea that all of us at Marriott are members of a team and that team members take care of one another.

Sometimes the assistance we give one another is nothing more complicated than covering for each other on the job to make sure everyone gets time off to attend special events and enjoy the holidays. Other times the helping hand is more dramatic. I doubt any of us at Marriott could tally the truckloads of food, clothing and necessities that have been collected, boxed up and driven thousands of miles to people in need in the aftermath of hurricanes, floods, fires, earthquakes and other natural disasters. When Hurricane Katrina slammed into New Orleans in August 2005, three of our hotels were flooded, and eight others felt the impact. As usual, associates donated money and personal leave. They, along with the company, our family and business partners raised more than $5 million for associate assistance and volunteered over five years to help rebuild homes, schools, and playgrounds. After a severe earthquake hit China's Sichuan Province in May 2008, one of our general managers led her hotel team in raising money, and including owners' donations, our total contribution was more than $3 million. Such generosity isn't unique to Marriott, but it's a gratifying reminder that caring for each other is a given.

The most touching stories I've heard are about Marriott associates giving support to colleagues living with serious illness. One team of associates at the Residence Inn® Asheville Biltmore in North Carolina banded together to help a fellow associate who had a child with a devastating disease. Others have helped out with sick spouses and elderly parents.

One of my favorite examples is two Marriott associates who took it upon themselves to look after a third who was dying of cancer. For more than two years, the pair dropped by the woman's apartment or hospital bed on a daily basis. On one of my visits to the area, I stopped by to say hello to the ill woman. Both of her friends were by her bedside. When she died about a year later, I had the honor of presenting the company's President's Award for extraordinary service to the two women who had shown such compassion for and devotion to their colleague.

These "put people first" stories I've mentioned involve associates helping guests or other associates. But the organization's DNA is also programmed to give our associates assistance. One of the most critical sources of support is training.

Every day, hundreds of our associates head for class-rooms and computers to upgrade their skills. From cooking and communications to teamwork and time management, you name it, we're probably teaching it. In addition to the growth opportunities these programs provide, specialized training paths give our managers the skills they need to manage our multigenerational workforce.

Marriott's commitment to training is common sense. We can't expect our associates to do their jobs well if we haven't shown them how. They deserve to know that the organization is willing to invest in building their skills and knowledge to give them more confidence on the job and a chance to keep moving up the ladder.

When we had our Hot Shoppes restaurants, all our managers and executives were trained to flip hamburgers, assemble salads and make sundaes by longtime associates who were experts at the job. And if the manager didn't pass the associates' exacting standards, he did not "graduate" until he improved. Period. No excuses. For many years we sent our chief financial officer and other nonoperations executives through the company's food school to gain a bit of hands-on experience with the products and services that formed the basis of Marriott's world. After we evolved into a lodging company, the learning shifted to how to clean rooms right every time.

I'm no exception to the learn-the-basics tradition. When I was an undergraduate at the University of Utah, I started out in the kitchen washing pots. I loved it. There was something intrinsically satisfying about seeing the stack of clean pots get higher as my shift wore on. Then they moved me over to the grill and the deep-fat fryer to make burgers and fries. That was fine until one afternoon when my boss told me to clean out the fryer, and then left me alone. I drained the fryer and then poured in hot soap and water.

Bad idea.

There was still a little hot grease in the fryer. The grease mixed with the soap and the water, and the resulting foam rose, and rose and rose. It bubbled up until it spilled out over the side of the fryer, all over me, and all over the floor. It took forever to clean up the mess. To this day I don't know if my boss simply didn't tell me how to clean the fryer, or if I wasn't paying attention when he did. At any rate, it taught me a lesson I've never forgotten. And it made me a diehard fan of training.

I particularly believe in exposing younger people to the

physically hard work that many of Marriott's jobs entail. Whenever I talk to students who plan to enter the hospitality industry, I underscore how critical it is to know the business firsthand, not simply as numbers on spreadsheets. Some graduates emerge from school thinking they're qualified to go straight into an executive slot. But if you don't know the business — the *real* business that your company does — you'll have a tough time grasping why one hotel or restaurant is doing better than another, or what the true cost of doing business is.

Besides training, we're big on providing support systems that let our associates know that they're not out there on the job alone, with no one to turn to for help if they need it. A good example is the process we use when we open a new hotel. Weeks ahead of time, a special team composed of veterans from other Marriott hotels takes up residence at the property to help the new staff debug systems, put on the finishing touches and roll out the red carpet on opening day. A skeleton crew sticks around afterward to help out until they're not needed anymore. All that fuss might seem like overkill, but I've yet to hear of a general manager at a new property who wasn't grateful for the support.

Another area in which we've invested is our work-life programs. Marriott is not the only large corporation to recognize the increasing complexity of modern life, but I'd like to think we're at the forefront of doing good things to help our associates cope with life's challenges.

Keeping our associates healthy and safe in the workplace is a top priority for us. In 2010, we launched Marriott's TakeCare — Choose Health Every Day wellness program to help our associates reduce stress and improve their health. In 2011, we expanded our Living Our Core Values/Living the Gold Standards program from the United States to include our properties in Asia. The initiative helps our associates with meeting basic human needs and improves engagement and retention.

One of the biggest challenges for Marriott has always been helping our associates juggle family responsibilities with duties on the job, particularly as more and more mothers and fathers both work outside the home. The task has become even more daunting as we've expanded globally and now have a workforce that is multinational *and* multicultural. Our associates speak more than 70 languages. In addition to language barriers, many must cope with complicated immigration procedures and interpersonal cultural clashes, not to mention the pressures of child care, elder care, or housing problems.

What toll do these problems take on our associates and, by extension, on the company as a whole? If your employees don't feel supported, they're not likely to give their best on the job. An associate who must scramble to replace a babysitter who canceled or who is worried sick about a recent call she received from an immigration lawyer isn't going to be in the best shape to deliver that all-important "human touch." What that troubled associate needs is a bit of the human touch herself, in the form of understanding and assistance.

In many cases, our associates help each other out. But for those times when colleagues and bosses aren't the answer, there are alternative sources of support. We provide an online and toll-free phone consultation service for our associates staffed by social workers who field questions and find solutions to just about any problem. And they can do it in more than 100 languages. We also offer financial tools for learning how to budget, figure out if you can afford a mortgage, save for retirement or your kids' education and navigate tax season.

Another long-term tradition at Marriott is our commitment to providing associates the opportunity to grow professionally inside the company. Thirty years ago, about one-third of all new Marriott managers were promoted from our hourly ranks. Today, the ratio is one in two. One former Marriott executive told me years ago that he thought the "genius" of our company lies in treating all our associates as if they were managers. I'm not sure I'd go quite that far — every organization needs leaders and followers — but I think he was on the right track. We believe all our associates have the potential to move up the ladder if they want to. When it comes to promotions, we'll always be more impressed by talent, hard work and dedication than paper credentials.

Bob McCarthy, our chief operations officer, is the first person to come to mind when I offer examples of opportunities at Marriott. Bob started working for us as a waiter when he was in college. After joining the company full-time, he worked his way up through various positions until taking over his current role in 2012.

Erica Qualls joined the company as an hourly worker in 1994, answering telephones on the night shift at one of our hotels. Today she is the general manager of the Atlanta Marriott Marquis, one of the company's largest hotels. Erica credits her success, in part, to the encouragement she received from leaders along the way.

Another success story is Liam Brown, who has been with Marriott for 23 years. When he and his wife emigrated to the United States from Ireland in 1989, they had just a few hundred dollars between them. He got a job managing a hotel in Massachusetts. We bought the hotel a year later and converted it to a Courtyard by Marriott®. Liam moved into managing several Courtyard hotels, and then a full-service hotel, before accepting a series of executive positions with responsibility for our extended-stay and select-service brands.

Nothing is as important as having managers in place who possess the people skills to support, encourage, lead, inspire and listen to associates. A manager without those skills is going against the grain of the organization and more than 85 years of corporate culture. He or she might be able to make good financial results for a short time, but in the end, the lack of people skills will always catch up.

Many years ago, on a property tour, I noticed that the new general manager of one of our hotels was making impressive numbers in his first nine months on the job, but the associates at the property seemed to me to be unusually subdued. Even the folks at the front desk — roles almost always filled by extroverts — looked uneasy.

Curious to get a glimpse of the associates at work when the boss wasn't around, I made a point of getting away from the GM for a short stroll on my own. I soon saw and heard enough to convince me that the whole staff was walking on eggshells. Closer investigation revealed that the associates were scared of the GM. He was bullying, punitive and unsympathetic to their concerns.

In spite of his recent good numbers, the manager was not good for the health of the associates. He didn't embrace our associates-first philosophy. The solution was clear: We had to let him go.

The true test of whether you put people first comes during tough financial times. Twenty years ago we were forced to lay off more than 1,000 people. It was one of the most personally wrenching periods during my half century with the company. Yet, in the end, the experience confirmed that our "put people first" philosophy pays off, even in bad times.

If you followed the business pages in the early 1990s, you might recall that Marriott went through some troubles from 1990 to 1993. The company had been on a roll throughout the 1980s — building hundreds of hotels, selling them to investors and negotiating long-term management contracts. We had hit on a formula for expansion that was tailor-made for the go-go times. By the decade's midpoint, we were one of the largest real estate developers in the country, accounting for one-third of all new hotel construction in the United States. In an average year, we handled about $1 billion in new construction. In 1989, we opened at least one new hotel every week.

Then the bottom dropped out of the U.S. real estate market in the fall of 1990 (the pattern repeated in 2008). That crash — together with a general economic recession, the outbreak of the Persian Gulf War early in 1991 and other factors — pummeled hotel demand and left us reeling. Lots of companies found themselves in the same boat when the economy stumbled. But we got caught in the middle of our ambitious expansion program with too much debt.

To pull ourselves back from the brink, we had to take a number of austere measures. One of the most painful was letting most of our hotel development & architecture and construction departments go. With real estate dead in the water and a backlog of hotels to sell, we didn't need — and couldn't afford — to keep idle staff on the payroll. Almost overnight, we had to close down the hotel development function. Thousands of planned hotel rooms were scrapped. Marriott had never before in its 63-year history faced the prospect of laying off so many people.

The only thing we could do was handle the layoff in a way that would take as much of the sting out of it as possible, for all parties — both those who were to depart and those who would stay behind. It was important to us to do our best to help all our associates cope with anxiety about the future. The people who were leaving deserved our support in finding other work, if possible, and the folks who stayed on needed to be reassured that their hard work was appreciated and they needn't waste energy agonizing over whether they, too, would soon lose their jobs.

The team responsible for handling the outplacement effort spent hours working out every possible option to help people prepare résumés, conduct job searches and deal with the stress of facing an extraordinarily tight employment market. Departing associates had access to professional counseling, interview coaching and office space where they could come each day to pursue job leads.

When the layoffs were announced, we braced ourselves. Not surprisingly, the anger of being laid off sometimes translates to litigation, and we had been warned that despite our efforts to provide for our associates, we weren't going to be immune.

The concern turned out to be groundless. Out of more than 1,000 people, only two took legal action against us, and those claims were minor and amicably resolved. In fact, I was touched when a number of departing associates took the trouble to thank us for our outplacement help. I was likewise pleased that we ultimately were able to help find opportunities elsewhere for more than 90 percent of those looking for jobs.

When we had to deal with the aftermath of September 11, 2001, and, more recently, the global economic downturn that began in 2008, we had the experience of the 1990s layoffs to draw on to handle the human side of the equation. Some layoffs were inevitable, but we were able to temper the pain by keeping many people on board at reduced hours but with full health benefits.

I believe the fact that the associates who had to leave us had enjoyed a good tenure at Marriott — had been, in effect, well taken care of — is what made the difference. Had those associates felt they had been treated carelessly during their years with us, I doubt we would have seen such understanding on their part. And those who remained at Marriott also witnessed the care and consideration given to their former colleagues.

It's this type of culture, treating people fairly and with respect, that has earned us placement on *FORTUNE* magazine's "100 Best Companies to Work For" list — an honor we've held every year since it was first launched in 1998. Of the awards we've garnered over the years, the ones that tell us we're doing a great job taking care of our associates are worth their weight in gold.

2

HE WHO LISTENS WELL
LEARNS MORE

*"It takes two to speak the truth —
one to speak, and another to hear."*

— HENRY DAVID THOREAU, essayist

Many years ago, a group of Marriott executives was waiting in our boardroom to update me on a hotel project I was particularly excited about. Senior-level representatives from all the key functions were there: feasibility, finance, design, construction, operations and the like. The group apparently killed time by talking about what an absolutely terrible idea the project was.

A few minutes later, I walked in the door, clapped my hands together enthusiastically and asked, "So, how's my project looking?"

Everybody responded, "Well, Bill, it's looking good, really good." Everybody except one fellow, a junior executive who had not opened his mouth.

Turning to him, I commented, "You haven't said anything. What do you think?"

He proceeded to rattle off all the reasons why the project was a disaster in the making — the same reasons that everyone around the table had been airing just minutes before I came in.

I paused a moment and then replied, "You know, you're absolutely right. Kill it."

I walked out. Jaws dropped around the table and that was the end of the project.

I tell this now classic Marriott version of "The Emperor's New Clothes" to make two points: One, most people will do anything to avoid being the bearer of bad news, and two, thank goodness there are a few hardy souls who won't.

Listening is the single most important on-the-job skill that a good manager can cultivate. A leader who doesn't listen well risks missing critical information, losing (or never winning) the confidence of staff and peers and forfeiting the opportunity to be a proactive, hands-on manager. Listening is also how you empower people to grow in their jobs and gain confidence as decision makers.

I'm convinced that there are few natural-born good listeners. Somewhere along the way, good listeners *learned* to be good listeners. I suspect they discovered that there are rewards for keeping your ears open.

Sometimes good listening simply requires keeping your mouth shut. It can be torture to hold your tongue and let someone else talk, especially if the talker is slow about getting to the point. In our company, people from all over the world work together every day, so it's particularly important to listen with patience and respect. Someone who is doing their best to express something in a language that isn't their native tongue deserves nothing less.

I've found it useful to mimic the body language of people whose listening skills I admire, people whom I enjoy talking to precisely because they listen to me so well. Great listeners have a knack for making you feel as if you're the only person in the world they want to talk to at that particular moment. President Bill Clinton is a well-known master of the art.

When you open your ears, open your mind, too. Listening is foremost an opportunity to learn. You won't learn much if you make up your mind before you've had a chance to hear anything. When my kids were growing up, I sometimes found myself talking at them rather than to them; even worse, I wasn't always listening to what they had to say. Any time I'm tempted to interrupt someone I remind myself that as long as I'm talking, I can't be learning about whatever the problem is. And if I don't know what the problem is, how can I expect to solve it?

My best experience in learning to listen well came in the mid-1970s when I served as bishop of my church for two years. In the Mormon Church, the role of bishop is a volunteer position that takes about 25 hours a week. In essence, I was the leader of my local congregation of more than 800 members, many of whom were people of very modest financial means. We talked over personal and family problems ranging from alcoholism to premarital sex to finding a job. To be of any use to them, I had to listen carefully and respectfully to their problems, from their perspective. After a few months in the role, I was standing next to my wife at church watching people file in and realized that I understood the burden or troubles that each person carried. I think those two years as bishop made me a better listener and a more compassionate person.

At the office I try to be careful not to signal that I've come to my own conclusions too early in a meeting. The less I say, the less I sway the discussion. I'd rather have people feel comfortable offering off-the-wall arguments or pie-in-the-sky concepts than take the chance that someone is holding back a good idea because they're picking up signals that the boss has already come to a decision. I especially want people to feel comfortable about raising red flags. If ever I need to be reminded of this point, all I have to do is think about how much money might have been wasted on a bad idea if that young executive had not spoken his mind that day.

A former executive once told me that one of the things he most appreciated about working at Marriott was the fact that he could promote and try to win support for his ideas up to the very end, the final vote. No one cut him off or shut him out before he'd an opportunity to make his best case, no matter how off-the-wall the idea.

A good example is our edgy lifestyle brand EDITION®. When the idea to team up with hotel designer Ian Schrager was first floated several years ago, the concept was definitely outside our comfort zone. Dismissing it would have been easy to do. Instead, we took time to listen to the pros and cons and gave ourselves permission to push the envelope. The result is a creative collaboration and a new hotel brand that will ultimately give us terrific sizzle in the marketplace, plus opportunities to be more playful and experimental as the brand rollout picks up pace in the future. Since then we've branched out with other novel hotel concepts like the Autograph Collection® and AC Hotels by Marriott^SM that might not have gotten a serious look a few years ago had we not been willing to give EDITION a fair hearing.

Occasionally, I've heard the criticism that I listen to too many people and seem to give equal weight to what each has to say, regardless of how knowledgeable or senior they are. Let me turn that criticism on its head. What message would I be sending to the organization if I gave an hour to finance, but only ten hurried minutes to human resources? Or if I never gave anyone under the senior vice president level more than 30 seconds of my time? I'd rather err on the side of hearing more than I might need to make a good decision and in the process give everyone an opportunity to be heard.

I've always believed in listening to the organization's heartbeat myself, instead of relying exclusively on my direct reports and senior staff for information. I call directly into our various divisions and levels to hear straight talk from associates. In part, the habit reflects my personal itch to be hands-on, but I also think the organization benefits from knowing that I'm accessible to more than my senior staff. And I benefit from having multiple points of contact in the organization.

It's critical to combat the natural tendency of staff to avoid telling the boss bad news or rocking the boat. Don't be afraid to ask questions in order to break through someone's hesitancy and get to the heart of a problem. It's a particularly important skill for presidents and CEOs who, merely by their lofty positions, often intimidate junior staff. I'm a great believer in the question "What do you think?" It works wonders. In fact, that phrase might just be the four most important words in business.

I must confess that I picked up that valuable tip directly from none other than President Dwight D. Eisenhower. My father and Eisenhower were great friends. While I was home on Christmas break from the Navy in December 1954, the president came to visit our farm in Virginia. At the time I held the lowest commissioned rank in the Navy: ensign. Here I was, in a family huddle with the commander in chief of the armed forces. We were all standing around the fireplace because it was bitter cold — below 20 degrees— trying to decide if we really wanted to brave the temperature to shoot quail.

Eisenhower looked around the room, then directly at me, and asked, "What do you want to do, Bill? What do you think we should do?"

I was stunned. I hate cold weather, so I said, "Let's stay in by the fire."

It later dawned on me that I had just witnessed firsthand Eisenhower's successful strategy for handling the huge egos he encountered during World War II. De Gaulle, Montgomery, Patton. None of them was a wallflower. He had been able to corral them as a team because he was willing to ask them questions and was interested in what they had to say. They knew he respected

I write about 700 notes a year to express my gratitude.

J. Willard Marriott, Jr.   10/30/07

Dear Mike —

I enjoyed my recent Tour of N.Y. With you. It was fun to have lunch in the associate cafeteria with you & to witness your great interaction with your people. You really know them all very well! You continue to do a great job and make us all proud. Thank you for a great day — Warm Regards Bill

Handwritten note to Mike Stengel, then vice president and market general manager for New York City's Marriott and Renaissance® Hotels, now Senior Vice President for Gaylord Hotels.

J. Willard Marriott, Jr.   10-24-11

Dear Erica —

It was great to see you at your fabulous Marriott Marquis — The Hotel looked great — you are an inspiring leader and Truly run a great Hotel — I'm proud of you and grateful for all you do! Warm Regards — Bill

Handwritten note to Erica Qualls, general manager of the Atlanta Marriott Marquis®.

These notes were used with permission from Mike Stengel and Erica Qualls.

them, so they didn't hold back their best ideas. Thanks to that fireside chat with Eisenhower nearly 60 years ago, I've always tried very hard to listen and ask questions.

———————

Today, social media makes it easy for organizations like ours to "listen" and ask questions of our guests. We're on all the popular platforms, from Twitter and LinkedIn to Facebook, YouTube and TripAdvisor, plus we maintain several blogs, including blogs for some of our brands like The Ritz-Carlton and Renaissance® Hotels. Our guests and associates have lots of opportunity now to let us know what they're thinking and how we're doing as a company.

I've been writing my *Marriott on the Move* blog since January 2007. Computers aren't my thing — I don't even know how to type — so at first I was a little dubious about the idea of having to come up with something new to say every day or so. But now that I've been blogging for more than five years, I can look back and appreciate that it has been an enlightening exercise in listening. For instance, I've discovered that personal stories and my musings about politics and current affairs tend to elicit more replies from readers than do entries in which I talk about things that the company is doing that might border on marketing or self-promotion. The blogs about my dog, Murphy, have been among the most popular.

The many blessings of technology notwithstanding, a long-standing practice that I won't give up any time soon is my habit of sending brief handwritten notes. I write about 700 handwritten notes a year — many of them to our associates, who have told me that they save them and look at them for motivation when things get tough. They're a nice counterpoint, I think, to the avalanche of emails and tweets that sometimes threaten to drown out simpler forms of communication.

I also answer nearly all the letters that come into my office from Marriott associates. If an associate takes the time to write me, he or she is owed a response. Usually, associates contact my office because they've got a problem or complaint that they want to bring to my attention. Small or large, the matter is investigated and we get back to them. I want to be sure that every Marriott associate feels that he or she can get a fair hearing. Even if the problem isn't resolved in the associate's favor, I'd at least like him to know that he received respectful attention.

Face-to-face meetings and anonymous surveys help us draw out how associates are feeling about their work, their job, their hours, their pay, their benefits, their general manager, their supervisor and everybody in the hotel. Part of the general manager's bonus is based on the associate engagement survey. The survey is as important to a general manager as customer satisfaction and profits. If a GM gets a bad score, he or she must fix the problem.

We count on our guests to tell us what we're doing right and wrong. It's the only way we can know for sure whether we're giving them what they want. Over the years, our guests have suggested many incidentals and small touches.

Today, electrical outlets are important. Our room designers used to bend over backward to hide outlets because they were ugly. That was fine before laptops, iPads, and smart phones. Today, travelers bring one or more gadgets with them and want to be able to plug in the moment they get to their room. No one wants to crawl around under desks or move furniture to find an outlet. So now we make sure that every room has plenty of them. If we hadn't been open to our customers' suggestions, we might never have known how much this one simple change meant to the comfort of our guests.

Anticipating a guest's needs is even better. One great story involves a group of marines who were displaced from New

Orleans when Hurricane Katrina swept through in August 2005. The marines were transferred temporarily to a Residence Inn® outside Atlanta. Two of them were supposed to have gotten married in New Orleans, but Katrina had forced them to cancel their wedding. During their three-month stay, the couple and the hotel staff became friends. When the pair decided to head to a justice of the peace to get married, they asked the general manager and the director of sales to serve as witnesses. On the day the ceremony was scheduled, the couple was taken totally by surprise when they saw the hotel's pool area transformed into a chapel and filled with more than 100 guests. Together, the hotel staff and the other marines had put together a beautiful wedding ceremony and reception for the pair.

I can think of at least one longtime executive who gained a reputation for being a poor listener toward the end of his career with Marriott. He never liked anything that anybody had to say. If someone offered a new idea, he would shoot it down with the same repetitive set of reasons: too much money, waste of time, too risky, whatever. Soon, no one wanted to tell him anything, because they knew what his response would be. He lost his credibility as a listener and, as a result, found himself cut out of substantive discussions and decisions. He forfeited the support of his people and finally lost his job.

Selective listening is almost as bad as not listening at all. You don't do yourself — or anyone else — any favors when you filter out bad news. Marriott learned that lesson the hard way at the end of the 1980s when we chose to downplay signals that the hotel industry was on the verge of being seriously overbuilt. We wanted so much to believe in our own invincibility that we focused only on positive news and turned a deaf ear to anything that we didn't want to hear. The price for that kind of half listening was high.

Our "it won't happen to us" attitude was exacerbated by the persuasiveness of one executive with considerable reassuring eloquence. His arguments were so smooth, so reasonable, so apparently logical that I let myself believe everything would be fine. But just because someone is a polished speaker doesn't mean that his or her ideas are always right. Conversely, someone who is a bit shy or awkward about speaking up might well be worth listening to.

Ultimately, even the most skilled listening has limits. Debate and fact gathering must come to an end. A decision must be made. This is the juncture at which the true mettle of an organization's overall listening skills is put to the test. If the environment for discussion has been an open one in which people know that their ideas, insights and concerns are treated with respect, the result will be well-informed choices. The team will be more likely to pull together to execute the plan. Not every decision will be perfect, of course, but when a decision does turn out to be wrong, there will be comfort in knowing that it wasn't wrong because someone forgot to ask the $64,000 question: "What do you think?"

3

ALL FOR ONE,
ONE FOR ALL

A lot of what I've talked about so far suggests that everyone at Marriott works cheerfully and unfailingly for the good of the whole. In general, that's remarkably true. Teamwork is a hallmark of our corporate culture.

At the same time, it doesn't mean that the company is filled with yes-men or people who can't think for themselves. Marriott's strong teamwork ethic just means that we've been able to create an environment in which the rewards for working together outweigh those of working for one's own interest.

How did we accomplish this? Before I get to that, let me tell you about a brief period in the company's long history when teamwork was not the order of the day. Although the situation didn't last long, the episode is worth highlighting because, for us, it was the exception that proves the rule.

The trouble stemmed from a rivalry between two particularly ambitious Marriott executives. The situation arose when the company underwent one of its periodic restructurings designed to give a few people the opportunity to try on new organizational "hats." Both men began eyeing the same hat.

Given the strong personalities of the two, I was prepared for a certain amount of friction, but the competition quickly took on the characteristics of a blood match, marked by heavy muscling and back-channel agendas.

It would have been bad enough if the negative impact of the competition had been limited to only those two individuals. But people who worked with or close to them got caught in the fallout of their machinations. Judgment, morale and productivity all suffered. No one — including the two executives — came out a winner. Neither got the position he was hoping for. Both eventually left the company.

The episode underscored a couple of fundamental truths. First, in a people-oriented business like ours, it's critical to get the "people" part right. Both of the executives were bright, capable managers, but instead of taking care of each other and those who worked for and with them, they let personal priorities get the upper hand. In the process, the pair destroyed goodwill, wasted energy and damaged morale.

The second truth illuminated by the contest of egos is that our corporate culture is at heart an egalitarian one. As an organization, Marriott has a low tolerance for big shots. An emphasis on title and privilege goes against our grain. Those who put themselves the most forward have been, in general, the least likely to get ahead.

When we were just starting out in the late 1920s, few, if anyone, in the company had special credentials. Everyone worked hard; everyone also had a fair shot at moving up the ladder. Dedication and street smarts were more likely to win someone a promotion than were academic degrees, the "right" connections or a knack for playing institutional politics. By the time American business became credential conscious after World

War II, Marriott's "everybody roll up your sleeves and pitch in" mindset was already a cornerstone of the company's culture.

Some of our attitude was just a reflection of the business we were in at the time: restaurants. While I was still working at the Hot Shoppes in Salt Lake City during college (scene of the infamous fryer-cleaning episode), I discovered that I thrived on the fast pace of the business. Teamwork was essential. When the noontime crowd poured in, everybody had to be at their command post and ready to go. If you didn't dish the food fast enough or if people weren't out on the floor taking care of customers, you would have a disaster on your hands. Getting ready for the 90-minute rush might take a morning's worth of planning and preparation. Everybody had to do their part. The whole system suffered if someone didn't show up for their shift.

Teamwork is especially vital when disasters hit. When Hurricane Wilma wreaked havoc on Cancun in 2005, many of our associates couldn't reach our hotel, the JW Marriott Cancun Resort & Spa. The ones who could get to work had to handle more than one job until their colleagues could return. The teamwork was phenomenal and made all the difference in getting the place back on its feet as soon as possible after the storm passed.

Many of our associates are "cross-trained"—meaning that they learn how to do jobs other than the one they're officially hired to do. Customers benefit immensely because they can approach almost any associate with a question or request and aren't going to receive "That's not my job" as an answer. Instead, the associate can either handle the request or knows how to find the right person on staff who can. Cross-training greatly improves the odds of having the right person at the right place with the right knowledge to help the guest.

Our associates benefit, too, from cross-training because the experience gives them the opportunity to try out different roles. The additional knowledge about the hotel's operations helps associates develop professionally and move up the ranks more quickly.

Because our business depends so heavily on teamwork and cooperation, we have a workplace that isn't a terribly comfortable environment for outsized egos or title seekers. Not that we don't have plenty of well-trained professionals in our ranks today. Nor does it mean that we don't have our share of superstar talent. We definitely do, including some exceptionally savvy people who have since gone on to other exciting challenges. While they were at Marriott, however, they were not handled with kid gloves.

Creating a teamwork-oriented culture is one thing; maintaining it is another. One thing that I think contributes to keeping the teamwork concept strong at Marriott is the fact that so many of our managers have come up through the ranks themselves. They know what it's like to be on the front lines. And they know how much *they* appreciated having a sympathetic and supportive manager early in their careers.

Another thing that keeps the teamwork principle alive and well is the fact that we're not willing to dangle outrageous incentive packages in front of talented people to keep them on board. We depend too much on people working together toward a common goal to risk fracturing the team by setting up a reward structure that distinguishes a few disproportionately. Everyone who works for the company is making a contribution to our success. There would be no quicker way to jeopardize, if not destroy, the we're-in-this-together ambiance of our workplace than by recognizing a few folks well beyond their market value.

Does that mean companies like ours have to forfeit the benefit of regular injections of superstar talent? Not at all. One of the most important, positive decisions a company can make is to welcome smart, ambitious people. Every business needs them to drive it into the future. What's important is whether or not the real go-getters know how to manage their egos. If they don't, the system must be strong enough to manage it for them. That means keeping a check on their ability to affect others adversely.

It's also important to promote an open environment in which everyone can be creative. Those executives who truly crave off-the-charts financial rewards will eventually leave anyway, but you'll still have plenty of others for whom the challenge of the job — the opportunity to be imaginative and to contribute — will be just as enticing as money.

If your company's structure and corporate culture are both strong, the institution should be able to withstand the comings and goings of ambitious people. You never want the organization to be held hostage by the creativity or drive of a single individual or small cadre of hotshots. In that sense, a healthy company is a bit like a good marriage. No one has the upper hand, special talents and contributions are respected and appreciated and all concerned know that the whole is worth far more than the sum of its parts.

As I've watched Marriott grow and change over the years, I've concluded that large companies must avoid allowing an organization's size to become an excuse for complacency, self-satisfaction, arrogance and passing the buck.

In an organization that has thousands of people and thousands of locations like ours, it wouldn't take much for bureaucracy to creep in and strangle initiative. Ideas can get lost in a maze of official channels. Associates can lose faith in their ability to make a difference, so they stop trying. Or figure someone else will pick up the slack if they fail to pull their weight.

One of the most effective counterattacks is to remind yourself constantly that your success didn't happen in a vacuum. Any thriving business needs people, both inside and outside, to make it a winner. We have literally millions of partners in our success. We have our team of associates, our most valued players. Then we have our property owners, our stakeholders, Wall Street, our industry colleagues, our franchisees and, of course, our customers.

You've already heard me say that our associates are number one. It won't hurt to underscore the point. Without their hard work, Marriott wouldn't exist. Period. That's why taking care of our associates is a top priority for the organization. It's also the reason why the kind of destructive personal rivalry that I talked about earlier is heartily discouraged and ultimately doomed to fail. Every single person who works for Marriott should be excited to be a member of the team.

How do you accomplish that goal when you have thousands of associates scattered around the globe? I talked a bit in Chapter One about some of the associate-oriented programs, initiatives and attitudes that Marriott has promoted over the years: training, work-life programs, a bias toward promotion from within. These visible signs all contribute — I hope — to sending our associates the message that Marriott recognizes that they're central to the company's success.

Recognition also takes the form of celebrating our associates' contributions. In 1996, we instituted an Associate Appreciation Day to remind everyone in Marriott on the same date, at the same time, that we're all in this adventure together. Parties, contests, special awards and genuine gratitude mark the day. It was so successful we expanded it to a full week the next year.

One special event that takes place in conjunction with Associate Appreciation Week is the Marriott Awards of Excellence ceremony. The Awards of Excellence, named after my father, honor our associates who go the extra mile on a regular basis. We've had associates from every walk of Marriott life win this honor: front desk clerks, van drivers, bakers, housekeepers, banquet assistants and so on. The Awards of Excellence program recognizes people in the organization who epitomize the best aspects of Marriott's culture. I particularly like the fact that the award recognizes our front-line workers in operations, not our executives. More recently we've added the Alice S. Marriott Award for Community Service and the J.W. Marriott, Jr., Diversity Excellence Award.

As important as companywide recognition programs are, it's even more critical to make associate appreciation a daily practice. Celebrating the successes of associates should be top priority for every manager. Sometimes a "Hey, great job!" is enough; other times, a larger gesture of thanks is called for.

Marriott's financial stakeholders are also partners in our success. Shareholders, leaders and other investors may not be as visible in the daily life of the company as our associates and our customers, but they are extremely important to us. Not only do they contribute the financing that makes it possible for the company to grow, but also they demonstrate faith in our ability and drive to make things happen. It never hurts to remember that no one is forcing people to invest in us — they ante up because we're committed to deliver.

When Marriott went public in 1953, our first offering sold out in less than two hours. If my father needed any assurance that his company was on the right track, that display of confidence supplied it. Six decades later, we still have a few of those original stakeholders, plus many thousands of newer ones, including associates who belong to the company's retirement savings plan. Our financial stakeholders provide us with plenty of incentive for doing the best we can to reward them with continued growth and consistently strong earnings. And as any public company knows, they'll be the first to let us know if we're disappointing them.

Competitors are also important to our long-term success, as they are often our best motivators.

When Marriott decided to go after the limited-service segments of the lodging market in the early 1980s, the specter of competition was a critical factor in our planning. We weren't too worried about the complacent companies that weren't likely to rally in response to Courtyard by Marriott. We were worried about what our nimble and aggressive competitors would do the moment we were out of the gate. Part of the excitement of Courtyard's development was the secrecy we maintained until we unveiled the product. The reward was knowing that many of the first guests at our Courtyard hotels were our competitors, checking us out.

Our turn to be surprised came in the late 1990s, when Starwood's hip boutique hotel brand W was unveiled. We and the rest of the hotel industry did a double take at the introduction of a sleek modernist product designed to appeal to younger urbanites with an appetite for minimalist décor but maximum style.

Just as our Courtyard by Marriott had been a game-changer in the 1980s, the introduction of W got everyone's adrenalin pumping. Our EDITION, Autograph Collection, AC Hotels by Marriott and revitalized Renaissance brands have been a multipronged response to customers seeking a lifestyle hotel experience.

We were also motivated by Westin's "Heavenly Bed®," introduced in 1999. Westin deserves full credit for beating us to the punch, but we like to say that we responded on a grand scale, by replacing and upgrading the mattresses and linens on more than 628,000 beds in the 2,400 hotels that Marriott managed or had franchised at the time. To give you a sense of scale, the global bed makeover used 30 million yards of cloth, enough to go two-thirds of the way around the world. Today, across all our brands, we're constantly dreaming up fresh ideas for our rooms, lobbies, restaurants and fitness centers.

Even while competitors are keeping you on your toes in the marketplace, keep in mind that they're also your peers. The old saying holds true: "What goes around comes around." If you hold yourself above your competition, you risk isolating yourself and losing out on sources of help when you need it most.

We work constantly with other hospitality companies to deal with local, national and global issues that affect our industries. Team effort takes place under the umbrella of our various trade associations. Many of us, for example, are working hard at the moment on boosting tourism to the United States, which nosedived after 9/11. When it counts, we pull together as an industry to educate government officials. That's how our industry was successful in getting Congress to pass the Travel Promotion Act that created Brand USA, the first global marketing program to entice more foreign visitors to our shores.

One of our most recent peer-level initiatives is a service called Room Key.com®, an online booking engine. We've partnered with Choice Hotels International, Hilton Worldwide®, Hyatt Hotels Corporation®, InterContinental Hotels Group® and Wyndham Hotel Group® to create our own search engine for travelers shopping for well-known hotel brands. RoomKey.com users can look for and book properties at not only all six hotel chains but also thousands of additional hotels.

Our owners and franchisees constitute yet another important set of Marriott partners. After a long history of being somewhat shy toward the lodging franchise community, we're thrilled to find so many opportunities today to ally with companies and individuals who want to be part of the Marriott family. Our partnerships with our franchisees really are partnerships; both sides make significant contributions to create and sustain the relationship. Among other things, our franchisees must share our bias for action, long-term vision and values, especially putting people first. They must be willing to live up to the same high standard of customer satisfaction that we expect of ourselves. To help them achieve that goal, we provide franchise properties with the same resources and support that we know from our own experience are critical to succeed, flourish and grow.

Every year, we honor our top franchisees with the Partnership Circle Award. My heart soars when I see winners such as H.P. Rama, a first generation immigrant from India, who has been a Marriott franchisee for 16 years. His son, D.J. Rama, worked at the front desk of our Providence Marriott while attending hospitality school at Johnson and Wales University in Rhode Island. He convinced his dad that Marriott would be the ideal partner for their family business, JHM Hotels.

It took H.P. and D.J. three years to qualify as a Marriott franchisee, but they were determined because they believed deeply in our values and corporate culture. They opened their first Fairfield Inn & Suites® in 1996. Today, their company has 42 properties, half of them Marriott brands, in the southeastern United States.

H.P. spends more time back in India these days, supporting a new generation of hoteliers at Auro University in Surat, India, which he created with the wealth he earned as a Marriott franchisee. Soon, the Ramas will open a Fairfield Inn on the campus, which now has 183 students studying business and hospitality.

I'm humbled when I think about H.P.'s story and Marriott's small part in it. After leaving his country to seek and find opportunity in America, he is returning to create opportunities for a new generation of Indian students, who will work in hotels that he hopes to open. And we hope he brands many of them Marriott.

Last but not least, among our partners in success are the millions of customers who use our services. We certainly wouldn't exist without the people who choose to stay in our hotels or vacation at our resorts. They have plenty of alternatives, and we know it!

Like our competitors, our customers keep us hopping. Part of what gets us out of bed in the morning is the search for new ways to keep them happy, earn their loyalty and win more customers. I'm the first to admit that providing food and shelter doesn't qualify as rocket science, but there have been plenty of things we've pioneered or tweaked over the years in the name of improving customer service. One of the most interesting evolutions, to my mind, is our frequent-stay program: Marriott Rewards®.

Our first program — Marriott Honored Guest Awards — was started in 1983 and quickly became the industry leader. The concept was pretty basic: Guests at our hotels, resorts and suites earn points for every visit. These points can then be applied to future room nights and other options. We complemented Honored Guest Awards with one of the industry's first frequent-flyer programs, Marriott Miles, which allowed guests to earn hotel points while flying. As we added limited-service brands, we added awards programs for each brand.

In 1997, we unveiled Marriott Rewards, which combined our separate incentives into a single program and has grown to more than 40 million members today. The program allows guests to earn points at almost any property in our system and apply those points to stays at almost any other — regardless of brand. In 2010, we introduced The Ritz-Carlton Rewards® program, allowing Marriott Rewards members to earn points at more than 70 Ritz-Carlton hotels.

The bottom line? Never take your stakeholders for granted. You only exist because of them. As Alexander Dumas' immortal Three Musketeers would say, "All for One. One for All. That is our motto."

PART II: PURSUE EXCELLENCE

"We are what we repeatedly do.
Excellence then, is not a single act, but a habit."

— ARISTOTLE
Greek philosopher and teacher

4

THE BENEFITS OF BEING
A HANDS-ON MANAGER

"It is not fair to ask of others
what you are not willing to do yourself."

— ELEANOR ROOSEVELT, First Lady

O n February 5, 2011, Ed Fuller, then Marriott's president and managing director of international lodging, landed in Cairo, Egypt, on a charter plane. Accompanying Ed were several Marriott associates. Less than two weeks earlier, on January 25, huge crowds had begun to assemble in the city's expansive Tahrir Square to protest the 30-year presidency of Hosni Mubarak. Dramatic images of milling protesters in Cairo and elsewhere in Egypt soon flashed around the world on television and the Internet. Within a week it was clear that the protests weren't going to stop — if anything, they were going to escalate. Violence was fast becoming a serious threat. At the time we had two hotels in Cairo and five more in the Sinai Peninsula.

When Ed and his team entered the Cairo airport, U.S. embassy staff were on hand, helping Americans who wanted to leave the country to fill out necessary paperwork and board departing planes. The staff naturally assumed that Ed and the others wanted to join the exodus. When he shook his head no, one of the embassy staff said flatly, "You are crazy."

Ed wasn't fazed. He's a Vietnam veteran, and during his 40 years with Marriott he has seen his share of revolutions. Ed and the team were anxious to visit our seven hotels in the area. They met with owners and reviewed and critiqued the security. Most important, they shook hands with associates and met with managers to listen to their concerns.

In Cairo — where we had 600 guests at the 1,200-room Cairo Marriott — the minister of interior removed all police from the streets and hotels. Even Ed, who has seen a lot in his travels, was blown away by what happened next. "Our culinarians came out and backed up our security staff with knives, while the housekeepers and engineers stood in line with brooms and shovels to hold the gates from the mobs," said Ed.

The hotel's owner, Chairman & CEO of Mirage Hotels Corporation Mounir Ghabbour, was grateful. In a letter to me, he wrote, "At a time when other Americans were leaving the country in no time, Marriott International sent their executives to support their owners and offer assistance. The approach left me speechless."

While Ed's decision to hop on a charter plane and race to Cairo isn't one that happens every day in Marriott's world, it's a memorable example of an attitude we value highly: the hands-on manager.

When I visit our hotels, I'm always looking for signs that the general manager is a hands-on manager. Does she radiate energy and enthusiasm? Does he know every inch of the hotel and grounds? How does the staff react to her? Does he know people by name (without cheating and looking at their name tags)?

The reaction of staff to the GM is the ultimate litmus test of how well a hotel is run. The same goes for any of our managers in any division of the company. If associates are happy to see the boss, I know that he or she is a great manager. Only someone who spends much of the day strolling the hallways or property talking to associates and taking their concerns to heart earns a genuinely friendly greeting.

If a manager is hands-on, more than likely she's also on top of her business. She can pick up immediately on problems, concerns or issues and take care of them before they fester or grow. Conversely, a manager who doesn't know his staff by name, who doesn't spend the bulk of the day walking the heart of the house, will eventually have problems. He's just not going to have the same rapport with associates or the knowledge base to make decisions as do his more engaged counterparts.

The management-by-walking-around approach became Marriott policy the moment the doors of our first root beer stand opened on May 20, 1927, in Washington, D.C. My father was the ultimate hands-on manager. He visited his restaurants almost every day, often with my younger brother, Dick, and me in tow. (Of course, as a kid, I just thought we were going out to eat.)

When we opened our first hotel — the Twin Bridges Motor Hotel in Arlington, Va. — in January 1957, we all pitched in. Mother, Dad, and I stayed up half the night hanging pictures so we could check in guests the next day in time for President Eisenhower's second inauguration.

When I took on the assignment of opening our second hotel — the Key Bridge Marriott in Arlington, Va. — in 1958, I was responsible for everything from hiring the architect and designing the hotel to securing the general contractor for construction to putting together the team we needed to get the hotel up and running on opening day. If I thought that in pulling off such a tall order I'd outgrown my days of picture hanging, I soon learned otherwise. The week before our first Philadelphia hotel opened on City Line Avenue in 1961, I was down on my knees gluing rubber baseboard into place in the lobby.

The time I spend on the road —some 60,000 to 70,000 air miles a year — visiting Marriott locations is how I stay connected to the business. One of the most important things it allows me to do is counter the notion that big corporations are faceless machines. It's important to me that our associates know that there really is a guy named Marriott who cares about them, even if he can drop by only every so often to personally tell them so.

I also want to show our team in the field that I value their work enough to take the time to check it out. Without their help, not only would Marriott not be Marriott; but also Marriott wouldn't be, period. I used to get down on the floor in hotel rooms and check under the beds. I open dresser drawers; switch on faucets, showers and lamps; and peek in closets to see if there's an iron and ironing board and enough hangers.

My visits are not limited to the public areas. I head for the heart of the house, too. I check out the laundry room, accounting office, kitchens, loading docks and any other corners that I think merit a quick look, including the associate break room. There's method to my madness. If I see smiling faces and well-scrubbed surfaces behind the scenes, I know that the rest of the hotel more than likely is doing just fine.

I rarely show up at Marriott locations unannounced. I often visit as many as ten locations in a single day, so I want to make every minute count. But letting people know that I'm coming for a visit occasionally has its humorous consequences. Over the years, I've learned to spot last-minute "the-boss-is-coming" freshening up, especially new coats of paint. I used to carry paint remover in my overnight kit to make short work of the inevitable streaks on my suits that result from good intentions.

My visits teach me volumes about what's working out in the field. I can't think of a single tour in all the years I've been on the road that didn't have at least one teachable moment or takeaway. I invariably return home with stacks of index cards filled with ideas about things that we should be doing or things that are out of whack and need fixing. (Yes, I'm one of a dying breed. I still write notes to myself and my team in longhand.) Those ideas quickly find their way into the hands of members of the team at headquarters who can either solve the problem or spread the word about a good concept that works.

Visiting Marriott locations year in and year out provides me with a strong knowledge base for making decisions. Because I'm involved in the day-to-day aspects of the business, our staff knows that if they come to me with a concern or idea, they're usually not going to have to spend a lot of time getting me up to speed. They can normally get my yea or nay readily and take action quickly.

One example is a decision we made to sell off the fine-dining operations of two food-service companies Marriott acquired in the 1980s. Marriott had been in the restaurant business for nearly six decades at that point and had had its own fine-dining operations in the past. I knew enough about the business from personal, frontline experience to know that we didn't want to wrestle with that category again. So when we purchased the giant food-service purveyor Saga Corporation for $700 million in 1986, we immediately sold off its restaurants for $350 million.

If we had not already had our own experience with fine dining, we might have lost time and a lot of money trying to make those restaurants work instead of quickly passing them on to someone eager to take them off our hands.

Sometimes it takes us a little longer to see the light. Our foray into senior living facilities is a great example. When we decided to get into the business of assisted living in the 1980s, it seemed like a natural extension of our lodging and dining experience. We care for people — that's our corporate mission. The housekeeping was similar to what we do in hotels: clean rooms, clean lobbies, mow the lawn, take care of the landscaping. And we figured we had the food service down cold after 60 years in the business.

What we failed to take into account early enough was the

health care part of the equation. Caring for healthy people in a hotel setting is one thing; caring for frail or ill people in an assisted-living situation turned out to be much more difficult than we thought. And seriously ill individuals — residents suffering from dementia, cancer or other conditions — had never been in our realm of experience at all. We didn't have the expertise to do justice to their special needs.

If we couldn't do it all and do it well, then maybe it was better not to do it at all.

Fortunately for Marriott, the assisted-living industry entered a consolidation phase right about the time that we decided to exit, so we were able to sell most of the small portfolio of properties that Marriott Senior Living Services had assembled to Sunrise Senior Living Inc., for whom senior living services is a passion. By late 2003, we were out of the business, wiser and really no worse for the wear financially.

Another benefit of being hands-on is what the marketplace can teach you free of charge. As I said in an earlier chapter, nothing replaces listening to your own customers firsthand. Not only will you find out what you're doing right and wrong, but also you might just pick up an idea for a brand-new product or business.

The incubation of Courtyard by Marriott in the early 1980s is a perfect example of how keeping your eyes and ears open in the marketplace can make for good business. Until Courtyard's debut, Marriott had focused only on the full-service hotel business. Other segments were new territory for us. When we decided to go after the moderate-priced hotel segment, we pulled out all the stops. Besides interviewing business travelers to learn what they wanted in a hotel room, we also checked out our competition by literally checking in to their hotels for a firsthand look. Our fanatically dedicated Courtyard development team spent hundreds of nights sitting in competitors' hotel rooms taking detailed notes about furnishings, room arrangements and service. The information the team gathered was critical to the fresh concept and design of Courtyard by Marriott.

More recently, the rollout of Wi-Fi services has provided us with a series of "teachable moments" in the art of keeping up with, or even ahead of, what the marketplace expects. Compared to the industry as a whole, we were early out of the gate in offering high-speed online access in our rooms. Because our Courtyard brand had been created specifically with the business traveler in mind, we knew that Internet and email access were competitive advantages. We purchased thousands of modems and cables to outfit our guest rooms.

As wireless services began to bubble up across the country and the world, we recognized the importance of staying on top of the trend. Consumers were getting used to Wi-Fi at coffee shops and other public places. They expected to find it in their hotels, too. We needed to deliver. By April 2004, more than 1,200 of our hotels offered free wireless high-speed access in their public spaces — the largest deployment in the hotel industry. Wi-Fi soon expanded to most of our rooms.

Today, the main Wi-Fi challenge is the question of how to keep up with bandwidth demand. Our data show that 40 percent of travelers carry two Wi-Fi devices, and 25 percent carry three or more. Guests expect to be able to upload and download huge data files, and watch television shows and movies, often at the same time. When you have a couple hundred people, or more, trying to do the same thing simultaneously in a large full-service hotel, it's challenging. Along with our colleagues in the hotel industry, we're busy figuring it out.

Although I'm not into electronic gadgets myself, watching the Internet explosion of the last decade has been fascinating for me. I see its evolution from the perspective of a businessman dedicated to giving customers what they want. While it is an incredible resource and tool, I still think it's not a substitute for face-to-face contact. That's why I'm out visiting our hotels as often as I can. And I expect our general managers to get out of their offices as much as possible. Companies that get into trouble are ones where the CEO never budges from the executive suite, and makes decisions without knowing what's really going on, because he isn't out in the field finding out for himself. You can't rely solely on reports or secondhand information. You have to get out there and find out for yourself.

At 80, being on my feet all day and running from location to location to stay on schedule can leave me wiped out at the close of business. But even as I'm easing gratefully into a hot shower at day's end, I know I wouldn't trade my time on the run for the most comfortable desk chair in the world.

5

DEVILISH DETAILS,
HEAVENLY RESULTS

"There is only one boss. The customer.
And he can fire everybody in the company from the chairman on
down simply by spending his money somewhere else."

— SAM WALTON, founder, Walmart

When my wife, Donna, and I were first married more than a half century ago, my father would visit our house and — like clockwork — run his index finger over the furniture, doorsills and venetian blinds checking for dust.

Needless to say, this drove my wife nuts.

I had it even worse. Donna merely married into Dad's perfectionism; I was born into it. My father was never satisfied with anything. Perfection was one notch below desired result.

When Dad visited the company's restaurants and hotels, he was always on the lookout. There was a specified way of doing things, and heaven help associates who caught my father's eye when they weren't following Marriott's standard operating procedures (SOPs). More than one Hot Shoppes cook, I'm sure, was stunned to find the chairman of the board standing by his side, testing him on how many times hash-brown potatoes should be turned on the grill. If the reply was anything but "once," you can bet my dad quizzed that associate to exhaustion about every other aspect of the job, suspicious about what other procedures the poor fellow might have been ignoring.

In the early days, before she had my brother, Dick, and me to raise, my mother also kept an eye open for ways to improve company procedures. On a visit to Salt Lake City to see her mother, she spent an entire day at the A&W root beer stand there. She wrote my father: "I found out that if you add some ammonia to the water when you wash these sparkling glass root beer mugs, that the mugs will be brighter and shinier and prettier."

Mom also inspected the soda-making machine: "There's a ball in the carbonation machine that must be washed at least three times a week and cleaned perfectly. Otherwise, it'll gum up the whole system." To make sure that he understood what she was talking about, she drew a diagram for him. She was all of 21 years old.

I'm more readily satisfied than my father ever was. But like him, I do believe that there's a right way and a wrong way of doing things — and doing things the right way is worth making a habit. True excellence includes taking care of the smallest details, even when they're not visible to your customers. If the devil is in the details, as has often been said, then that's clearly where it pays to pay the closest attention.

We are sometimes teased about our passion for the Marriott "way" of doing things. We're known in the hotel industry for our detailed procedures. The aim is to provide our customers with service free of hassles and surprises. We could not have expanded as quickly, widely or profitably as we have over the years if we had had to reinvent the wheel every time we unveiled a new hotel or resort, or if we were forced to reintroduce ourselves to the world each time a new property opened. Many guests at our newest hotels come to us because they've already experienced Marriott elsewhere. Customers probably don't spend a moment thinking about it, but our SOPs are part of what bring them back.

When I came on board full-time in the mid-1950s, my first job was in food service. My main task was to continue to beef up our service standards. I had just completed a tour with the Navy as a supply officer, but Marriott still had plenty to teach me about efficiency. I spent the first few months on the job figuring out how to eliminate slow-ups in Hot Shoppes service due to lack of plates, dishes, silverware and so on. My job also included a constant hunt for ways to shave seconds off the time it took to process a food order, from the moment it arrived in the kitchen to the moment a waitress served the dish to the customer.

My budding career in food service ended abruptly when I asked Dad to let me get involved with managing our brand-new Twin Bridges Motor Hotel. His initial response was a no-nonsense "You don't know anything about running a hotel." To which I replied, "Yeah, but neither does anyone else around here." Thus began my career in hotels.

Maybe I should have been more daunted by our lack of experience in lodging, but truth be told, it was fun. In contrast to Hot Shoppes, systems were few and far between on the hotel side of the business. We were flying by the seat of our pants, thrilled and a little surprised by our own presumption. My recent tour of duty aboard the *USS Randolph* — essentially a floating hotel — definitely came in handy.

We didn't start out modestly. Twin Bridges was a sprawling complex of 365 rooms — so big that we hired bellmen on bicycles to guide guests in their cars to their rooms. Our second hotel, Key Bridge, had more than 200 rooms to start. Seemingly before the original paint dried, we added more rooms and public spaces to both hotels and began planning our third and fourth.

We were able to transfer a few systems from the Hot Shoppes to the hotels, but it was really the transfer of attitude about systems that counted most. The whole time we were experimenting with our first few hotel properties, we were also diligently jotting down every idea that seemed to work, slowly building from the ground up not only our hotels but also the systems to run them.

I remember starting room service from scratch at Twin Bridges, about four months after the hotel opened. Talk about a making-it-up-as-you-go-along experience. At the end of my first month on the new job, I found myself putting together room service trays and filling guest orders myself. Not that I was any kind of expert on the subject. I quickly trained two or three other people, and they took it from there.

Keeping costs under control was another challenge. My very first "executive decision" involved, of all things, ice buckets. I was looking over our expenses for Twin Bridges a few weeks into the operation and noticed a sizeable sum under the category "Other." A little investigation revealed that guests found our plastic-covered, cardboard ice buckets so sturdy and convenient that they were filling them up with ice and drinks to take on the road. At $1 apiece, the loss of thousands of buckets in a year would have quickly eaten up our meager profits. (Average room rate in 1957 was $9 a night.) It might sound laughable now, but the solution was simple, I ordered permanent metal ice buckets to be placed in each room, guests refrained from taking them and we were back in business.

Today, of course, we're far more sophisticated about finances. We have plenty of administrative systems to monitor every aspect of our operations. In fact, we've set the industry standard for tracking RevPAR, or revenue per available room, a method for evaluating how well a hotel is doing financially.

Nonetheless, even the most cutting-edge financial and accounting systems wouldn't have gotten us very far if we hadn't had something to sell to our customers.

Marriott's principal product is probably not what you think it is. Yes, we're in the lodging business. Yes, we sell room nights. But what we're really selling is our expertise in *managing the processes* — especially how we welcome our guests at check-in — that make those room sales possible. And that expertise rests firmly on our mastery of hundreds of tiny operational details.

That's important because our successful track record and experience in *managing* hotels is what attracts the investors who actually *own* almost all the hotels that bear our name. And those investors are critical to our growth around the world.

Are you surprised that Marriott doesn't own most Marriott hotels? We used to, when we started our lodging division back in the 1950s. At that time, we had just a few hotels. But from the late 1970s until the early 1990s, our primary growth in lodging came from building and selling hotels to investors and then agreeing to long-term management contracts to run the hotels. By 1997, Marriott owned outright only about a half dozen of the more than 1,500 hotels that carried the Marriott logo. By the time we reached our goal of 2,000 hotels in 2000, our proportion of ownership was less than 1 percent of the hotels in our global system. Today, only a few hotels are actually owned by Marriott International.

Many additions to our lodging system in the past two decades have come from franchising the various Marriott brands. We weren't always so enthusiastic about the idea of allowing our name to be on a building we didn't own or manage. My dad saw what had happened to the Howard Johnson® chain in the 1930s and 1940s when it franchised its restaurants widely and lost control of the situation. Among other things, the company failed to enforce strict, uniform standards of maintenance, food and service. As a result, HoJo®'s restaurants went downhill and cost the brand name its halo.

Dad's reluctance to franchise kept Marriott out of the game in a serious way until the 1990s, with good and bad results. The downside of waiting so long to take a whole-hearted plunge into franchising is that we missed out on valuable expansion opportunities for a couple of decades.

The upside is that the delay gave us ample time to develop a solid track record as an operator. Affiliation with the company's brand is more valuable to our franchisees now than it might otherwise have been. We were also able to develop systems to help our franchisees deliver strong results. And we've had the opportunity to develop truly franchise-friendly select-service brands like Residence Inn by Marriott®, Fairfield Inn & Suites by Marriott®, SpringHill Suites by Marriott®, Courtyard by Marriott®, and TownePlace Suites by Marriott® — all of which are relatively easy to run compared to a full-service hotel. Franchising works well for us. I'm proud that you can't tell the difference between a managed or franchised hotel when you travel.

This is a long way of saying that Marriott's major selling point — the fuel for our growth since 1978 — has been our ability to show investors and franchisees that we know what we're doing when it comes to running a hotel. That's where the hash browns, room service and ice buckets, plus hundreds of other details, come into play. Our intense attention to detail translates into consistent quality. Consistent quality leads to high customer satisfaction. Customer satisfaction translates into high occupancy, repeat business and good room rates. Those in turn bring home good profits and attractive returns to property owners and franchisees.

Our operational skills are what saved us when the hotel industry ran into trouble at the beginning of the 1990s, after 9/11 and during the 2008 – 2010 economic downturn. In order to ride out the economic storms of the past two decades, we had to maintain customer and investor confidence in our fundamental strength as an operator. Our talented folks in operations, plus our tried-and-true systems, produced consistent results in customer satisfaction.

Now that I've praised systems and SOPs, let me talk about what they don't do. Even the most detailed procedures can't cover every situation, problem or emergency that might arise.

A guest who gets sick in the middle of the night doesn't want to wait around while a desk clerk looks up the right SOP for the situation. She just wants to get to the hospital. The same goes for a guest who left his passport in Room 1308 and is now calling from the airport, panicked about making his international flight. He just wants compassion and speedy assistance.

One of our regular guests wrote me a few years ago to share a story about a front desk associate at one of our Courtyard hotels near St. Louis, Mo., who, to her awe, juggled four tasks simultaneously: fixing the uncooperative printer in the business center, checking in a steady flow of guests, answering the front desk phone and chatting with the computer help line people on a second phone. The associate heroically crawled around on his hands and knees under the printer desk, checking cables, stopping every so often to stride quickly back to the front desk to help someone else. Never once did he stop smiling and — most important to the guest — never for an instant did he make her feel as if she was a problem. When she grabbed her printed document and ran off shouting, "Thank you!" he just grinned and waved. For him, spontaneous multitasking was simply all in a day's work, not the result of memorizing an operating manual.

Not long ago, a family stayed with us at The Ritz-Carlton on Amelia Island, Fla. When they returned home, they discovered that their son's beloved stuffed giraffe, Joshie, had somehow been left behind. To comfort his distraught son, the father told him that Joshie was taking an extra-long vacation at the resort. Fortunately, the hotel found the giraffe in the laundry room and called to let the family know. Relieved, the father asked if they'd mind taking a picture of the giraffe sitting by the pool, to corroborate the vacation story. A couple of days went by, and a package arrived from the hotel. In it was Joshie, together with some Ritz-Carlton-branded goodies, plus a binder that documented Joshie's extended stay at the resort, complete with pictures of him sunning himself by the pool, getting a massage, riding in a golf cart and even taking a shift in front of the security monitors as an honorary member of the hotel's Loss Prevention Team.

Needless to say, the parents were thrilled by the creativity and kindness of The Ritz-Carlton staff. The father blogged about the family's experience and the story appeared in several places on the Internet. Joshie the Giraffe even scored his own Facebook page.

Our other brands also love to offer our guests the kind of personal attention that makes the difference between a satisfactory stay and a memorable one. Our SpringHill Suites brand, for example, sponsors a nationwide, month-long celebration of local artists every September. During ArtNight festivities, guests can enjoy original works of art in a gallery setting, meet the artists and savor local music.

Our Renaissance Hotels brand offer Navigator, an on-site, online and mobile program that provides guests with a carefully compiled database of recommendations for local food, spirits, retail, music, entertainment and culture. An on-site Navigator can also work one-on-one with a guest to create a personalized visit — a service that maximizes the guest's time to enjoy local hidden gems.

Early in my own career, I received an unforgettable lesson about customized service and customers. While in college and still working at the Hot Shoppes in Salt Lake City, I got promoted to fountain service. If you wanted to survive, you learned very quickly what made the waitresses happy and what made them mad. Questioning their orders fell into the latter category.

While working the fountain one night, I glanced up when one of the waitresses put a slice of pie up on the shelf in front of me and said, "I want this a la mode."

"Fine," I replied, reaching for my ice cream scoop.

"I want brown gravy on it, too," she said.

"What?"

"Apple pie with ice cream and brown gravy."

I must have looked at her as if she'd lost her mind because she leaned in, looked me straight in the eye and said meaningfully, "That's what the customer wants. So that's what the customer gets. Right?"

Who was I to argue? I gave him apple pie, ice cream and ... brown gravy.

6

DECIDE TO DECIDE

"The unfortunate thing about this world is that good habits are so much easier to give up than bad ones."

— W. SOMERSET MAUGHAM, novelist

few minutes before 10 a.m. on October 2, 1989, I hurried aboard an Amtrak train at Union Station in Washington, D.C., for a three-hour trip to New York City. The miserable rain outside mirrored my mood. I had been awakened by chest pains in the middle of the night and had not been able to go back to sleep. Instead, I'd gotten up, popped a couple of aspirins, pedaled my stationary bike for a few minutes and headed to the office before 6 a.m.

As I settled into my seat for the long ride, I was still feeling lousy.

Two minutes before we were due to pull out of the station, I grabbed my briefcase and hopped off the car, my chest on fire. Bracey, my driver, had stuck around, in case I didn't make the train. I jumped into the backseat, and he raced to Georgetown University Hospital.

Over the course of the next three months, I suffered two more heart attacks and underwent a coronary bypass operation. Counting time in the hospital and time at home recuperating, I was out of commission for the better part of six months.

When you're going through something as dramatic as a heart attack, you tend to think that a mistake of gigantic proportions has just been made. Someone else — not you — is supposed to be lying in this particular hospital bed, staring at the ceiling or watching an IV drip.

In my case, there was no mistake; I was exactly where my bad habits had put me. For years leading up to my heart attacks, I had been the walking stereotype of the workaholic executive: too little exercise and rest, too much work and too many heavy dinners too late at night. By the third heart attack, I concluded that if cardiovascular trouble didn't kill me, my wife probably would if I didn't make some changes in the way I was living.

Most of the adjustments I made were the standard ones we've all heard about. I made the typical dietary changes, cut back on travel a little bit, began exercising regularly on a treadmill and picked our lakeside home in New Hampshire as the relaxing place to visualize when I need to calm down during stressful moments.

The most difficult change by far was attitudinal. Not only did I inherit my father's workaholism and heart problems, but I also picked up his habit of worrying. While Dad was alive, he frequently handwrote long notes to me in the dead of night because he literally couldn't rest until he'd gotten whatever was bothering him on paper. Night-shift associates at our properties would do a double take when they spotted the chairman walking briskly through a hotel kitchen at 3 a.m., wide awake and raring to go. Dad paid for his perpetual restlessness with an ongoing series of illnesses that sometimes took him away from the office for months at a time. My mother spent a great portion of her time nursing him back to health, only to watch him lose it again to work and worry.

I've never been quite as bad as my father. On the other hand, I probably didn't learn as much as I should have from his up-and-down state of health. Or at least, I didn't learn until I got waylaid by serious illness myself. Like my dad, I have a hard time sitting still when there's work to be done. (And there's always work to be done.) Over the decades, I definitely have had a rough time not worrying about the millions of things, large and small, that can go wrong at Marriott.

The irony, of course, is that my heart attacks only brought more worries. One of the worst aspects of the illness was the timing. In the fall of 1989, some of the signs of bad economic times that I mentioned earlier were becoming hard to ignore. Being upset by the unpleasant thought that I was sidelined just as we were perhaps about to encounter some of our biggest challenges didn't speed my recovery either. It was also not easy to face the fact that three decades of 16-hour days on the job had put me in the very position I most wanted to avoid: not being at the helm if we hit rough seas.

Rough seas or not, my body told me in no uncertain terms that I had to slow down, take it easier and make some fundamental attitude changes — or risk getting socked again with another heart attack. One critical attitude adjustment I made in the aftermath of illness was to become better at delegation. I still chomp at the bit waiting for results from our team, but I no longer have my hands in everything that goes on in the company. My penchant for being hands-on remains as strong as ever; I simply don't exercise it.

One of the most valuable lessons that my heart attacks taught me was to improve the balance in my life between work and play. I *thought* I had things in balance while my four kids were growing up, years before my heart attacks. I made it a point to be available to help them with homework, talk through a problem and cheer them on at school events. If I wasn't traveling, I was home by 6:30 p.m. for family dinner, even if I had to go back to my desk later in the evening. On weekends, we visited museums and battlefields, attended sporting events in Annapolis, Md., and more.

75

My heart attacks in 1989 showed me that I didn't have things quite as balanced as I thought. So I made a commitment to draw a bigger, bolder boundary line between work and home. My wife, Donna, and I have a standing "date night" each week to give us time to decompress together. We usually head out to the movies — alternating between fast-paced thrillers (my choice) and "chick flicks" (Donna's choice). And, of course, we've taken lots of wonderful family trips together around the world.

A better balance also meant working harder at saying no to demands on my time. Naturally, family, our church and the company take precedence, in that order. Invitations to just about everything else are frequently and politely turned down. Saying no is hard for me, but I must.

I also added Pilates to my regimen. I try to work it in twice a week. My wife and daughter-in-law had told me I was "shrinking" and needed to do Pilates to get my posture and stature back. They keep telling me it has improved my posture, but I'm skeptical. I do think it's made me more flexible. For an old guy, I'm pretty flexible. It's stimulating and it's kind of fun and I enjoy it. I wouldn't want to do it seven days a week, however. I still prefer my time on the treadmill, five times a week; a habit I developed after my heart attacks.

Why have I told you this? If even one person learns from my life-threatening experience, changes his or her habits and is spared a heart attack or other stress-induced illness, I'll be pleased. Anyone who thinks that pushing the limits of human endurance is necessary to a company's success should think again. The pursuit of excellence in business shouldn't come at the price of good health and well-being nor at the cost of family and friends. My heart attacks merely made everyone worry, from family to friends to associates to Wall Street. Work hard by all means, but don't run up a huge tab of stress and worry. Sooner or later, you will pay for it, and so will everyone around you.

The other personal lesson that I want to share is one that came early in my adult life and fortunately didn't require the drama of a heart attack to sink in. I learned it while growing up in my church, the Church of Jesus Christ of Latter-day Saints, also known as the Mormon Church. Former Church President Spencer W. Kimball termed it "deciding to decide."

For me, it meant that as a young man, I concluded that I simply wouldn't do certain things, like be unfaithful, smoke, drink alcohol or use drugs. I chose to put my family first, then my church, then my business. And I decided that that would be the last time I'd have to make a decision about those particular temptations or personal priorities.

As 19th century philosopher Thomas Carlyle once said, "A man lives by believing something, not by debating and arguing about many things." Once you decide to decide, life becomes surprisingly simple. You don't have to think about certain issues or questions again. You simply get on with things and don't waste time and energy rehashing — debating and arguing — the problems and possibilities.

Speaking purely from my own experience, a personal decision to make family a top priority can be tremendously gratifying. My happiest moments are those spent with my wife, Donna, our children; our grandchildren and great-grandchildren. Mormons believe that families stay together for eternity, so we tend to view the family circle as the central source of daily support in our lives, in good times and bad. We laugh together, pray together and give each other a boost when we're down. In a world that often seems bent on self-destruction, the security of a close-knit family provides riches beyond compare.

Deciding to decide and then sticking to those decisions has another benefit. No doubt I sound old-fashioned, but I think there's satisfaction to be had in standing firm against the onslaught of temptations that are part and parcel of contemporary life. Saying no consistently can provide a sense of real power in a world that often seems out of control. Not everyone finds the idea of hard-and-fast choices appealing, but I've found it liberating. It can also keep you humble by providing an ongoing reminder that no one's judgment is so infallible that a few rules aren't necessary. I can say in all honesty that I've never met a happy playboy.

Both ideas I've touched on in this chapter have to do with recognizing personal limits. In the case of my heart attack, I learned that the old saying about robbing Peter to pay Paul has dangerous consequences. I stole from my health in order to satisfy my workaholic habits. For my trouble, I almost missed watching my grandchildren and great-grandchildren grow up.

Recognizing my limits was a pivotal factor in my decision in December 2011 to step down as Marriott's chief executive officer. I'm confident that Arne Sorenson will do a terrific job.

Remember what I said earlier about not letting an institution be held hostage by the presence or absence of a single individual? While lying on my back in a D.C., hospital in 1989, I had learned that Marriott the man might be felled by illness, but Marriott the company has a constitution of iron. Our executive team had stepped up to the challenge of my absence beautifully. I would have been devastated if our company had fallen into disarray or paralysis simply because I was out of commission for a few months. As much as anyone likes to think he or she is indispensable, it was gratifying and comforting to see Marriott's organizational maturity and teamwork come through in what could have been a crisis.

In the years since my heart attacks, I've had plenty of opportunity to ponder and choose the best way to guarantee that my presence or absence would never be a deciding factor in the health and well-being of the company. I've been in the saddle long enough (more than a half century) that I could easily have contracted Founder's Syndrome. We all know the type: the hard-driving workaholic who dies at his desk; the 92-year-old patriarch who won't give up the reins to the younger generation; the founder who keeps so much vital information to herself that when she dies, the company falls apart within months.

I can understand how hard it is for someone who has built a company from scratch and has a tough time hanging up his spurs. My dad had a tough time handing off responsibilities to my brother, Dick, and me. Of course, the company was much smaller then. Today, a global company like Marriott with $12 billion in reported revenue in 2011 is so big and complex that I would have been fooling myself if I thought that I could — or should — control every aspect of our operations. Besides literally working myself into the ground, I would have been setting up the company — my life's work — to fail. That's not something I could imagine doing. And so, years ago, I decided two things: I would make sure that we always had plenty of executive bench strength. And I would step down, with no hesitation and no regrets, when I knew in my heart that the time had arrived.

When that moment came in December 2011, the news of my retirement as CEO was greeted as we hoped it would be: as a natural outcome of a succession-planning process that has been under way for years. But the announcement also qualified as "big news" in that, for the first time, someone outside the Marriott family had been chosen for a role that is the most high profile in the company. For the first 85 years of Marriott's history, the CEO slot had been held by only two men: my father, then me. That's quite a run.

The decision to step down wasn't difficult for me. My 80th birthday was on the horizon, and I honestly don't believe that anyone who is 80 should be running anything. Most companies have a mandatory retirement at 65. A lot of CEOs are retiring in their 50s, some of them in their early 60s. I had been CEO for 40 years, and I decided the company needed a younger person to do the day-to-day stuff that a CEO needs to do.

From the moment the transition was announced, Arne and I both received hearty congratulations, as well as plenty of questions about how the decision came about. It would make for more dramatic telling if I could say that I had a fireworks-and-marching-band epiphany while sitting on my dock in New Hampshire at sunset or while watching Arne deliver a flawless speech to a group of financiers. But, in all honesty, the choice of Arne was a gradual process, an evolution.

I recognized Arne's talent immediately when I first met him back in the early 1990s. He was a private litigator then and worked with us on the split of the company into Marriott International and Host Marriott. I asked him to come on board to head up mergers and acquisitions. At some point I found myself listening to Arne's ideas with more than ordinary interest. He had a good grasp of the company's strengths and weaknesses, a feel for the future of the travel industry and a sense of direction that impressed me and others. Not to say that he was alone in having those characteristics, but Arne definitely stood out. He also seemed to "get" our values and culture — key for anyone who might lead the company someday.

I know many people expected one of my four children to be a natural successor. That's understandable. Debbie, my oldest child and only daughter, is a hard-charger in her role as head of Marriott's government affairs, but she has been in the role only a few years, after spending the last two decades being a full-time mother. Stephen, my oldest son, has his hands full dealing with a rare medical condition that has slowly robbed him of most of his sight and hearing. My youngest son, David, works for the company, but he's still young and would need plenty of time and experience to grow into such a big job.

My second-oldest son, John, seemed the most likely candidate in the eyes of many observers. And I won't say that he wasn't put through his paces to see if the role might suit him. He made the rounds of company operations both here and abroad.

But John is a born entrepreneur. He thrives in an environment that isn't chockablock with four- and five-hour meetings, which is what a lot of the CEO role entails. I was sad when John opted to leave the company a few years ago, but he's happier doing his own thing. To spend the better part of your life doing something you don't love is not the ticket to happiness. It's more likely to lead to ulcers and disenchantment.

Among other pursuits, John manages the family's real estate investments as chairman of JWM Family Enterprises, which he founded. Plus he's vice chairman of Marriott's board of directors and he heads up a successful medical testing start-up. So even if we're not working side by side on a daily basis, we sit next to one another at our board meetings. I think that getting the question of succession out of the way has made us better friends. And he no longer has to put up with the scrutiny that comes with having Marriott as a last name.

Arne, too, was given different responsibilities around the company to see how he thrived in various roles. He was our chief financial officer at one point and also spent some time as the head of our European lodging operations. The board of directors and I have watched him handle the strain of 9/11, various overseas crises we've faced plus the economic downturn, and I came away feeling confident that he was a great choice for CEO. By the time we announced the decision in December 2011, he had been handling some of the CEO-level duties for a couple of years, so stepping into the role officially wasn't difficult for him. He has the blessing of our board and the Marriott family and has been well received by Wall Street, our shareholders and our partners. We really couldn't have asked for a smoother transition.

PART III:
EMBRACE CHANGE

*"The art of progress is to preserve order amid change
and to preserve change amid order."*

— ALFRED NORTH WHITEHEAD
mathematician and philosopher

CHAPTER 7:
PRESERVE ORDER
AMID CHANGE

CHAPTER 8:
PRESERVE CHANGE
AMID ORDER

7

PRESERVE ORDER
AMID CHANGE

*"The rung of a ladder was never meant to rest upon,
but only to hold a man's foot long enough
to enable him to put the other somewhat higher."*

— THOMAS HUXLEY, biologist

In June 1997, Microsoft's Chief Technology Officer Nathan Myhrvold uttered one of the most famous premature epitaphs in American business: "Apple is already dead."

Apple® Computer Inc. was the brainchild of Steve Jobs and Steve Wozniak. After making a big splash in the 1980s with its Macintosh personal computer, the 21-year-old company was on life support. Steve Jobs had been pushed out of the company in 1986 in favor of a less volatile leader.

A month after Myhrvold's pronouncement, Jobs returned to Apple and began applying the corporate equivalent of CPR. Apple soon dominated the digital music space, reinvented the Mac and, in 2007, brought out a snazzy new smart phone that sent other phone makers scrambling to catch up. Devotees couldn't get enough of the reborn company's products. When the iPad debuted in April 2010, it almost singlehandedly created today's multibillion-dollar tablet market. On August 10, 2011, Apple Inc. ended the trading day with a valuation of $337.2 billion, squeaking past Exxon Mobil to enjoy the rank of most valuable company in the world.

Apple's amazing roller-coaster ride from the company's birth in 1976 up to the death of Steve Jobs in October 2011 is probably the most spectacular business turnaround in history. It's also a case study in the dangers of not managing growing pains proactively. Alfred North Whitehead neatly sums up the ideal: "The art of progress is to preserve order amid change and to preserve change amid order."

While Marriott hasn't had the made-for-Hollywood boardroom dramas of Apple, we have had our share of moments when the balance between order and change got out of whack. In my long tenure, I've seen Whitehead's paradoxical statement play out over and over in our company: To grow successfully, you must stay true to who you are, even while working feverishly to *change* who you are.

First, "preserving order amid change." Between 1927 and 1957, when we opened our first hotel, Marriott's financial picture grew from the original $6,000 that my father and his partner, Hugh Colton, borrowed and pooled to more than $36 million in annual sales. The only year that didn't bring an increase in earnings was 1942, during World War II. After we entered the lodging business in 1957, growth continued at a rewarding pace. We hit $1 billion in annual sales in our 50th anniversary year, 1977. Just before we encountered the problems of 1990, we enjoyed an unbroken string of a dozen years in which annual growth hovered around 20 percent.

Twenty percent, in fact, became a magic number for us. We began using the shorthand 20/20 to sum up our annual growth goal: 20 percent growth in sales and 20 percent return on equity. The catchy phrase gave our large, far-flung organization an easy-to-remember mission and a sense of "order" amid the topsy-turvy growth. One former Marriott executive was always impressed that our frontline associates, located thousands of miles from corporate headquarters, could reply "20/20" when asked what their goal was for the year.

During periods of rapid change, it can be easy for an organization to fall out of step. Marriott's first major order-change imbalance came in the late 1960s. In 1968, we announced that we would begin franchising Marriott hotels on a limited basis. The fact that we were franchising at all was itself a major change for Marriott. As I mentioned earlier, my father disliked franchising, because he objected to not having day-to-day control over the management of his business.

Marriott really fell down on developing the systems we needed to make our initial foray into franchising work. First, we jumped in too fast and had to beat a hasty retreat when we found that we had far too many unqualified applicants trying to give us a check in exchange for a Marriott franchise.

No sooner did we get a handle on the application process and narrow the field than we inadvertently tripped ourselves up by deciding that the franchised Marriott hotels — to be called Marriott Inns — needed to be distinguishable from the company's own hotels. From today's standpoint, the decision is a strange one; one of the strengths of franchising is to have all properties be part of one seamless system.

We soon realized that we weren't ready for franchising and backtracked a bit along what had been proudly touted as a new avenue of growth for Marriott. We scaled back our ambitions, opened fewer franchised hotels and, in general, moved far more slowly than originally planned.

Know-how wasn't the issue. Marriott's management systems are so strong that we would have found the right answers and gotten ourselves well organized before too long. Franchising was new to us, but running hotels was not. The real problem was one of mindset. As an organization, we simply didn't embrace franchising as wholeheartedly as we needed to make it a success. Even as we jumped into "change" enthusiastically, a key component of our "order" resisted adapting to and supporting the change.

Today, we've thoroughly embraced hotel franchising. The most important shift has been in our attitude. Once we decided to think of ourselves as a franchiser — and made that mindset an authentic component of our day-to-day operations — the rest fell into place. In fact, today we actually franchise more hotels than we manage.

One of our most successful franchisees is Bruce White, whose hotel business, White Lodging, was at a critical juncture in 1985 when he reached out to Marriott to franchise a Fairfield Inn & Suites in Merrillville, Ind. Without an iconic brand behind him, his hotels weren't earning the profits that justified the sweat and tears, and he couldn't attract the financing to grow his business.

I admired his entrepreneurial spirit and knew Marriott needed to use other people's capital to grow our distribution, so we took the plunge and he became our first Fairfield franchisee. Today, White Lodging manages more than 200 hotels — including Courtyard, Residence Inn, Fairfield Inn & Suites and SpringHill Suites properties, and many full-service properties, including the spectacular JW Marriott Indianapolis and the new JW Marriott Austin which is under development.

Bruce says Marriott taught him how to be a great service organization and transformed his small company into a thriving business. We've learned from Bruce that we can franchise even large luxury hotels, if we have the right partner.

Our initial experience with franchising wasn't limited to the lodging side of the business. We gave it a shot on the restaurant side, too, with our Roy Rogers and Big Boy chains, which we acquired in the late 1960s. Both purchases took us into the unfamiliar territory of restaurant franchising. We stayed with the businesses for the better part of 20 years, but we frankly did not embrace franchising any more fervently on the food side of the business than we initially did in lodging. In part, we were hampered by certain provisions in the original Big Boy purchase agreements. But mainly, it was another instance of not being ready to think of ourselves as a committed franchiser. The result was that we really didn't grow the businesses as aggressively as someone else might have. We got out of both Roy Rogers and Big Boy in the late 1980s.

In the meantime, it became increasingly clear to me that we needed to make another critical change if we wanted to keep growing: Our corporate financing philosophy needed a drastic overhaul.

For the first 50 years of our existence, Marriott had sported a "bean counter" mentality toward finance. Property leases and traditional mortgages were pretty much the extent of our financial universe. As long as we were leasing and building small facilities like restaurants, our simple financing approach was adequate.

But by the mid-1970s, when we were trying to move into the big leagues, the traditional formula was holding us back. We were especially hampered on the lodging side of the business, where the price tag for a single convention hotel could easily run into the tens of millions of dollars. Significant mortgage debt not only limited the number of hotels we could build, but also put a real strain on what we could show in the way of returns to our shareholders.

So, beginning in 1978, Marriott revolutionized its entire approach to the lodging business. The single most important element of the change in philosophy was one I've already mentioned: our decision not to be a hotel ownership company, but to focus instead on being a hotel *management* company.

The most visible impact of the decision was seen on the company balance sheet almost immediately. We began by selling to investors several of the hotels that we had built before 1978. As part of the deals, we signed long-term management contracts and retained a significant part of the cash flow from the properties. No longer held down by heavy mortgages, we gained more financial flexibility.

The next revolutionary change involved turning ourselves into a major real estate developer, but with a firm commitment not to retain the real estate. Why wait around for others to build hotels and ask us to manage them when we could construct them, sell them, and keep long-term management contracts? Why wait to be invited to the dance when we could build the ballroom and hire the orchestra ourselves?

Marriott's organization responded to the call for development capacity by setting up a huge construction pipeline. The company had long had an architecture and construction team, but the scale of building would be supersized compared to anything we'd done in the past. Feeding the pipeline would also require much more complex financing resources than Marriott had been accustomed to dealing with.

Creative financing ideas were soon bouncing around our boardroom, aided and abetted by major changes in the federal tax code in 1981 that fueled real estate development in general. To grow as planned, Marriott had to transform itself into a deal-savvy organization. Once again, our "order" adapted to the change. We found ourselves easing into the let's-make-a-deal mindset that characterized much of 1980s business. Our legal and finance departments quickly mastered the intricacies of syndications, limited partnerships and other real estate investment vehicles.

Large-scale deal making meant debt. My father had always viewed debt as an evil to be avoided at all costs. He had watched his father, Hyrum Marriott, lose everything in the Depression of 1919, on the heels of World War I. Borrowing money was anathema. But to achieve the magnitude of growth that would move Marriott to the next level, debt financing was vital. I talked; he listened; he grimaced; I borrowed. The company's sense of "order" adjusted yet again to fit our new needs.

The three D's—development, deals and debt — came as a package and brought fundamental, institutionwide change to

Marriott's order in the 1980s. The organization largely dealt well with the growing pains that came with change (we eventually sold more than $6 billion in hotels in the 1980s), but not without a bit of stumbling.

The upside is that when we popped out on the other side of the real estate crash in the early 1990s, we had built some of our most spectacular hotels: the Atlanta Marriott Marquis, the New York Marriott Marquis and the San Francisco Marriott Marquis. These iconic hotels became brand builders, establishing Marriott as a large, significant hotel company.

We also possessed a much more sophisticated financial skill set and a keen appreciation for the merits of not getting so far ahead of ourselves. Although I wouldn't relive those days for anything, I'm proud that our company's "order" absorbed the hard lessons of overextending ourselves and adjusted accordingly. As a result, we weathered the financial challenges of 9/11— in part because of then President George W. Bush's support to bring travel back — and subsequent economic turmoil without losing our footing.

That's not to say that we haven't experienced disappointments or have called every shot correctly. Recessions still take their toll. Not every financial relationship we've entered has worked out as planned. And not every hotel in every location makes its numbers 100 percent of the time. We won't hit the ball out of the park every time we swing, but that's OK. My comfort is that even the maestro, Steve Jobs, didn't get *everything* right.

Besides keeping the corporate mother ship steady on the financial front, there are other aspects of our existing order that it would pain me to see become casualties of change. As I'm sure is crystal clear by now, the most important one to my mind is our corporate culture.

Maintaining an organization's core culture takes work. Especially so when you've grown from a handful of local restaurants into a huge, multifaceted, global enterprise. Size alone makes it a challenge to communicate meaningfully with associates working at thousands of locations around the world. Fortunately, as we've expanded, so has the Internet and other methods of real-time communication. Compared to just 20 years ago, we can reach out with amazing speed and depth to our associates wherever they are around the globe.

Marriott is not only geographically dispersed but *culturally* diverse as well. Our nearly 3,800 hotels are spread out in more than 70 countries — many of which are home to cultures whose sensibilities can differ markedly from one another. A wide range of languages, customs and world views are represented among both our associates and our guests. We value diversity as one of our strengths, but it does demand a special consciousness and sensitivity to extract the full benefits.

For one thing, we've learned that not everything translates perfectly or with ease. Our "put people first" core value, for example, requires no explanation to Americans who have been raised in a culture that champions individual initiative. For people who grew up in cultures that put the accent on group achievement — not individual effort — the idea is harder to embrace. Our teamwork ethic might come naturally to those associates, but the idea of being competitive or aspiring to promotion can be quite foreign and even uncomfortable.

That's where our general managers play an incredibly important role. It's in their hands to train and support associates so they can grasp and embrace Marriott's culture with open arms. As our company grows ever more global, we'll need more and more general managers who have come up through the ranks, understand the market, understand our culture and know how to help other Marriott associates around the world understand and embrace it, too. This outreach applies to franchised as well as managed properties.

We recently restructured the company into four geographic regions, a major change for us after more than 80 years of being run almost entirely from our Bethesda, Md., base. From the outside, the restructuring might not seem like a big deal, but for a company that has had its heart and brain anchored in a single spot for decades, it represents an important shift in mindset.

On one level, the change is simple pragmatism. By pushing decision making closer to the field, we empower our managers and associates to do what works best locally.

On another level, it's an acknowledgment that Marriott now boasts a truly global footprint as a company. We're comfortable anywhere in the world. Best of all, we're not simply exporting a well-vetted American product and plunking it down wholesale in another country. We're learning how to tweak our spaces, our service, our offerings to appeal to a truly global audience while reflecting local culture, tastes, history and more. I've been in this business my whole life and I'm still amazed by some of the bold architecture and one-of-a-kind designs of our hotels, not to mention the different guest experiences we offer.

I doubt that many of our guests will notice our global reorganization on a day-to-day basis. That's as it should be. But in the big picture it will empower us to offer our guests the finest combination of broad global reach and authentic local flavor.

8

PRESERVE CHANGE
AMID ORDER

"It is not the strongest of the species that survives,
nor the most intelligent, but the one most responsive to change."

— CHARLES DARWIN, naturalist

In the preceding chapter, I talked about the challenges that Marriott has faced in transforming itself from a small local company into a large global one. Our growing pains reflected one-half of Alfred North Whitehead's proverb about progress: the task of preserving order amid change. Time for the flip side: the job of preserving change amid order.

Given the speed of change today, there might not seem to be anything worth saying about the need to preserve it. In the 85 years since Marriott opened its doors, the world has been altered almost beyond recognition. My parents went into business the day Charles Lindbergh began his legendary transatlantic solo flight — May 20, 1927. The Roaring '20s were in full swing. Calvin Coolidge was president. My mother, who lived into her 90s, saw the sound barrier broken, people walk on the moon, the human genome deciphered and space shuttles orbit the globe. That's just a razor-thin slice of life in the realm of science and technology; changes in politics and society have been revolutionary, too.

Change can be exciting but brings with it the potential for

error and embarrassment. One of the best lessons Marriott has taken to heart over the years is that of not letting ourselves be crippled by mistakes. Instead, we look for a useful takeaway and move on. If you don't move on, "order" gets the upper hand, and before you know it, the only change being experienced is that of going out of business.

Naturally, change is easier to handle if you're the one initiating it. But in business — as in life — you're not always the one in the driver's seat. Competitors can be coming at you from all sides, forcing you to step on the gas to stay ahead. Or you're the one speeding up to catch somebody else who's gotten out in front of you.

Marriott has experienced both scenarios. We've had another compelling reason for embracing change over the years as well. As a public company, Marriott has to show our stakeholders that we can produce results. That means that we need to be willing to be a "creative disrupter" — a trendy term in business management circles — of our own status quo. In brief, we need to shake ourselves up once in a while.

If you're under the age of 40, you might not know much about the non-hotel businesses we've had in the past. There have been quite a few. Our first foray came 10 years after the first Hot Shoppes opened in 1927. The In-Flite airline catering division was launched in 1937 when my father noticed customers taking hot coffee and food "to go" from one of our Hot Shoppes near Washington's Hoover Airport. During the next 50 years, we built the division from the original contract with Rickenbacker's Eastern Air Transport into a more than $1 billion business before selling it in 1989. Along the way, we grew In-Flite by building flight kitchens ourselves and acquiring a number of independently owned kitchens and small catering companies. One of the most important things that In-Flite did for us was diversifying Marriott in international terms. Our first overseas operation was a flight kitchen in Caracas, Venezuela, acquired in 1966. At its height, In-Flite had kitchens in 20 countries.

The next diversification effort was more dramatic, because it took us beyond restaurants and catering. After nearly 30 years in the food business — Hot Shoppes, In-Flite airline catering and food-service management — Marriott launched into the lodging business with what we proudly dubbed the "world's largest motor hotel" in January 1957, four years after the company went public.

The site for Twin Bridges was just south of Washington, D.C., on Route 1, close to Reagan National Airport, the Pentagon, a bridge across the Potomac River and other major transportation arteries. The location we selected was not by chance. My father loved to put his Hot Shoppes at busy intersections and, when possible, near bridges. He reasoned that highways might be relocated, but bridges never move.

The groundwork for Twin Bridges was laid when my dad opened a Hot Shoppes on Route 1 at the entrance to the 14th Street Bridge in 1936. In 1950, he purchased a large piece of land just across the highway, with an eye toward building a new central office, food-preparation facility and warehouse for the Hot Shoppes. But our executive vice president, Milt Barlow, told Dad that he thought the site had great commercial potential. Why not build a big motel, he suggested. After all, 125,000 cars passed by the spot every day, the airport was close, the Pentagon was next door and downtown Washington was only five minutes away. In short order, plans for a 365-room hotel were drawn up, and we entered the lodging business in 1957.

Success was spotty at first. In the 1950s, the hotel business tended to be seasonal. Twin Bridges would fill up with tourists in the spring and summer and empty out in the fall and winter. So we built a ballroom on top of one of the guest room wings and turned an unfinished basement into a meeting room for conventions. The first group we booked had more than 400 people. In the early 1960s, a businessman complained to me that he couldn't get a proper drink in Virginia — restaurants were prohibited from selling liquor until 1968 — so we followed the accepted protocol of the day and opened a private club where drinks could be sold. (Though Mormons don't drink, as a businessman, I'm not going to tell others that they can't.)

Twin Bridges had a pool that was drained in September. During the winter, it was dead space. We decided to freeze over the whole area and open a skating rink. We unwittingly provided our customers with free entertainment. Diners came to the hotel's restaurant to enjoy the spectacle of skaters falling down on the ice.

Key Bridge, which we opened in 1959, also took time to get traction. It took us a little while to develop enough marketing muscle to bring in a steady stream of commercial business and small conventions to keep our rooms filled year-round.

Considering our complete lack of experience, we were incredibly lucky with our first two hotels. Part of our luck was pure timing. Our lodging business was launched when the American hotel industry was still recovering from World War II. Lodging options for travelers consisted mainly of old city hotels built in the financial heyday of the 1920s or hundreds of tiny mom-and-pop motel operations. When we appeared on the landscape with Twin Bridges in 1957, we were just smart enough to know we had something fresh to offer and just naive enough to go at it with the wide-eyed enthusiasm and energy of a bunch of kids who knew nothing about the business.

One thing our good timing brought us was a little breathing room to figure out just what the devil we were doing. When I look back, I have to laugh at how little we knew when we were starting out in lodging. Thank goodness most of our competitors were as new to the business as we were. Otherwise, they'd have eaten our lunch.

Dad in front of the first Hot Shoppe in 1927. He'd be thrilled his little venture became a global brand with 3,800 hotels in 70-plus countries.

Here I am on a hotel tour in the late 1960s with my sons Stephen and John. I have fond memories of Dad doing the same with me.

Hot Shoppes grew into a regional restaurant chain. That's me in the driver's seat, circa 1950.

I talked my dad into letting me run our first hotel, the Twin Bridges Motor Hotel in Arlington, Va., which opened in 1957. To keep business thriving in the winter, we converted the swimming pool area into an ice-skating rink.

FAMILY FIRST

Marriott Family

Family portrait taken in 1949 of me (standing); my brother, Dick; and my parents.

Marriott Family

Taken at my wedding, in 1955, to the love of my life, Donna.

Marriott International

Dad and me, 1972, the year I became CEO of the company.

Gale Frank-Adise

My pillars of pride, my children — David, Stephen, Debbie and John — in front of a replica Hot Shoppes counter. I'm happy to say they all contribute to the company's success.

FAMILY FIRST

The Marriott family in 2011. Donna and I are thrilled to have four children, their spouses, 15 grandchildren and seven great-grandchildren in our family.

INNOVATION

Blake Marvin

Our purchase of The Ritz-Carlton® Hotel Company in 1995 immediately solidified our position in the luxury segment. This picture of The Ritz-Carlton, Half Moon Bay near San Francisco, Calif., says it all.

Marriott International

Courtyard by Marriott® was a major innovation — the first moderately priced hotel brand for the business traveler, promising a good night's sleep at a good price, with Marriott quality.

Shelby Studios, Inc

With Autograph Collection® — a group of independent hotels — we quickly entered the boutique hotel space. Pictured is The Cosmopolitan™ in Las Vegas.

Jeff Zaruba

The New York Marriott Marquis® is a global landmark now, but when it opened in 1985, Times Square was not the tourist hot spot it is today. This hotel continues to be one of our most profitable.

Nikolas Koenig Photography

We have big plans for EDITION®, the new lifestyle brand we are rolling out with Ian Schrager. Shown here — The Istanbul EDITION®.

Leibmann Photographik

We opened our first European hotel in 1975. The Amsterdam Marriott is still open and was recently renovated.

Marriott International

The recently opened JW Marriott® Cusco is our newest and oldest location. The hotel opened in 2012, and the site dates back to the 13th century, when Cusco, Peru, was the Incan capital.

Marriott International

When we open our first sub-Saharan hotel in 2013, the Kigali Marriott, we will employ 15 graduates of the Akilah Institute for Women as supervisors.

Tom Luddington

The St. Pancras Renaissance® London Hotel is a fabulous hotel and one of the city's greatest landmarks. It opened in 2011, and the beautiful architecture, art, design and décor embrace guests with British history.

GLOBAL GROWTH

Andrew Loiterton

Since 2012 most of our growth has come from outside of North America. Pictured is The Ritz-Carlton®, Hong Kong.

Geoff Lung Photography

I attended the opening of Pune Marriott Hotel & Convention Centre in India, and there was glitz, glamour and green. This hotel is luxurious and has LEED (Leadership in Energy and Environmental Design) Gold certification.

Marriott International

The tallest hotel in the world, the JW Marriott® Marquis® in Dubai, which opened in late 2012, will not disappoint travelers seeking the ultimate in hotel luxury.

SERVE OUR WORLD

João Tezza

Over the last five years, we've contributed $2 million to protect 1.4 million acres of rainforest in Brazil.

Marriott International

Following the devastating earthquake in Haiti in 2010, our associates with ties in the country encouraged us to build a hotel there. In 2014, we will open the Haiti Marriott in collaboration with the Digicel Group and the Clinton Global Initiative.

SERVE OUR WORLD

Through the Bridges program, Cristal Sanchez landed a sales job at Kohl's. Each year, Bridges...From School to Work® helps more than 1,000 young people with disabilities prepare for the workplace and find jobs.

As we grow in countries outside the United States, we will continue our tradition of being engaged in the communities where we build hotels. Here I am at a Habitat for Humanity build in Washington, D.C., in 2004.

While on a hotel tour in China in 2011, Arne Sorenson made a stop in the Sichuan Province, where we are helping farmers cultivate honey as a sustainable economic alternative to other ventures that cause erosion and degrade the water supply.

PUT PEOPLE FIRST

Marriott International

We continue to recognize our best associates for outstanding service every year with an award named for my father, the J. Willard Marriott Award of Excellence. Additional awards celebrate community service and commitment to diversity.

Stephen Grande Jr.

Whenever I visit a property, I remind our associates that they are what makes the Marriott experience so memorable. Here, I thanked associates from New York's Essex House, which returned to the Marriott portfolio as a JW Marriott in 2012.

Marriott International*

When we added Gaylord Hotels to our portfolio recently, I personally welcomed our newest associates to our team in person.

LEADING IN CRISIS

Managing through 9/11 and its impact on our hotel, our people and our industry was definitely a test of leadership for me. Shown here: the Marriott World Trade Center hotel and the Twin Towers, prior to the attacks.

I have worked with several presidents, most recently Barack Obama, to champion the travel and tourism industry in the United States. Travel is an export — when people travel, they spend their money, which creates jobs and boosts the economy.

LOOKING FORWARD

Marriott International

I was completely overwhelmed and touched by the outpouring of gratitude and support I felt at our Full Service General Managers' Conference in March 2012, when I formally stepped aside as CEO while remaining executive chairman.

Ben Hider

In May 2012, Donna and I rang the closing bell at the New York Stock Exchange, along with members of our family and the executive committee — a symbolic moment for our company, which was celebrating its 85th anniversary.

Tiffany Photographic, Inc.

I couldn't be more pleased that Arne Sorenson is leading our company. He's the right man to propel us on our path of global growth and brand innovation while remaining true to our core values.

Marriott International

In the Pilates studio with the "Wunda Chair." I plan to keep up with my Pilates.

Had I had my way, we would have plowed our energy into building the hotel division faster and sooner than we did. I felt confident that the future promised to be a bright one for new, aggressive hotel companies. Change was all around us. The interstate highway system was growing, new office buildings dotted the suburbs, commercial airports were popping up and general postwar prosperity was kicking up a tidal wave of business and leisure travel.

But Dad and Wall Street had other things in mind. At the time, my father was still set against taking on the scale of debt required to build a lot of big hotels. Wall Street was crazy about conglomerates; analysts constantly wanted to know what new business we were getting into next. So in the early 1970s, we began looking around for additional avenues of growth outside of restaurants and lodging.

So in the spirit of diversification, we created Marriott World Travel, a travel agency launched in 1971. The business played to several of Marriott's strengths and seemed to be a natural outgrowth of our existing businesses. We had a dozen hotels at the time and would soon have three cruise ships and two theme parks. With leisure travel on the upswing, a travel agency seemed perfect for Marriott.

So what was the problem? Probably the most important sticking point was the distinct displeasure of established travel agencies — many of whom could and did quickly stop sending clients to anything related to Marriott. In retrospect, we should have anticipated the potential for conflict. The original team in Marriott World Travel was also a bit too ambitious for our own good; they committed Marriott to various initiatives and weren't able to follow through. The change they were trying to implement was a little too precocious. We gave the travel agency business a good effort, but exited in 1979.

The next diversification opportunity came in the shape of

cruise ships, a business we got into in 1972. Sun Line provided our first major lesson about the dangers of getting into a completely unfamiliar business. Having diversified successfully and relatively painlessly into hotels 15 years earlier, we felt confident that we could pull it off. After all, cruise ships were basically just floating hotels, right? Isn't that what I had learned in the Navy on board the *USS Randolph*?

Wrong. Not only was the cruise ship business more complicated than we realized, but we also made the error of getting into a partnership in which we didn't have the controlling interest. It drove us crazy not to be calling the shots. It didn't help matters that the Greek islands — the main destination of our ships — were plagued by the Cypriot War our second season. For obvious reasons, tourists prefer not to cruise in a war zone. Before the war started, our ships were full; after the shooting began, cancellations poured in and we had to tie the ships up right at the peak of the cruise season. We spent 15 years trying to make a go of it before finally getting out.

At the same moment that we took on the Sun Line challenge, Marriott decided to get into the theme park business. Our foray into theme parks, unlike cruise ships, was to be a bottom-up effort. We planned from the start to build them ourselves and not partner with anyone.

Theme parks took advantage of several of our strengths. We grew up in the food service business, were fanatical housekeepers and were definitely family oriented. For our two Great America theme parks, we picked high-traffic locations in the San Francisco Bay Area and midway between Milwaukee and Chicago. We slated openings to take advantage of the Bicentennial fervor of 1976.

Our first hard lesson came during construction. Building a park from scratch without any previous experience turned out to be both tricky and expensive. We had become experts in designing and constructing big buildings — our full-service hotels — but small one-of-a-kind structures that had to conform to another category of building code temporarily threw us for a loop. We had never built a roller coaster, for example; eventually, we constructed six. As soon as they got the hang of it, Marriott's architecture and construction division did a terrific job. The buildings and rides at both parks were wonderful.

Our big mistake with the theme park business was not recognizing the amount of money and imagination required on the entertainment side of the picture. Adding new rides is extremely capital intensive; a single ride costs several million dollars. Really good rides — the kind that bring people in by the droves — also require an edgy kind of creative thinking. Plus, the weather can have a big impact on this type of business. After several years of doing well, but never feeling entirely comfortable with the business, we sold the properties at a profit and bowed out.

Cruise ships and theme parks were our biggest and most expensive diversification efforts of the 1970s, but not the only ones. One venture that I would gladly forget is our brief excursion into selling home-security systems. It only lasted three years — from 1973 to 1976 — and, fortunately, was little more than a blip on Marriott's radar screen. A more recent example is HomeSolutions, a home-cleaning business that we launched in the late 1990s and later wound down. Neither business fit us.

The silver lining of our short-lived explorations into unfamiliar businesses is the lesson it taught: the importance of letting people develop new ideas. These particular ideas themselves didn't work for us, but we discovered that our organization is flexible enough to try novel concepts and resilient enough not to let failure get in the way of giving other ideas a fair shake. I call that preserving "order amid change" *and* "change amid order" at its best.

In all the diversification efforts mentioned so far — with the exception of hotels — I've noted that we discovered major, ultimately insurmountable, difficulties only *after* getting into the business. One of the most valuable lessons we learned in all those ventures — aside from the importance of taking risks and bouncing back — is that when problems arise in a business, you need to know enough about the business to be able to fix them. It's that simple. If you don't understand the business in the first place, you can't fix it when it goes wrong. In fact, you might not even be able to figure out what the problem is.

In each case, we were guilty to varying degrees of not having done enough homework before plunging in. So we were blindsided by problems that might have been avoided or that would have alerted us to steer clear of the business altogether.

What we experienced during that period was simply a growing pain common to businesses trying to extend beyond their original ideas. Our enthusiasm for innovation occasionally got ahead of our organization's ability to manage it. Among other things, we were trying too many unfamiliar businesses simultaneously.

What was missing at Marriott in the 1960s and 1970s was an organizational structure for analyzing and managing change. Until the late 1970s, my father and I looked at business opportunities on a case-by-case basis. Our informal decision-making methods were in keeping with the company's traditional approach to growth. For the first 30-odd years of our history, the primary strategic question was by and large limited to picking the right location for a new Hot Shoppes. When we jumped into airline catering in 1937, the strategy still revolved around location: up-and-coming airports for our flight kitchens. When we got into lodging in the mid-1950s, we were still focused on the same basic question: Which suburban markets, convention cities and major transportation hubs did we want to target?

The "location, location, location" planning mindset was ideal for building our food and lodging divisions but fell short of what we needed to analyze new, unfamiliar businesses. Looking back,

I see now that the case-by-case approach was partly a reflection of our long-standing orientation (some would say bias) toward operations.

We assumed too confidently that there wasn't anything that the company's first-class operators couldn't ultimately figure out how to run. What we learned, of course, is that even the very best operators can't fix a decision that wasn't right in the first place.

By the late 1970s, it was time to acknowledge that Marriott needed to be more disciplined about analyzing potential business ventures. In 1977, we established a strategic planning department. To some degree, we were merely following the trend in business management. But for Marriott, it was also an important step along the road to organizational maturity. We liked change but had not adjusted our organization to *manage* change for our benefit. By harnessing change, the strategic planning department simultaneously protected — or preserved — the organization. We took a leap toward achieving the all-important balance between order and change.

Marriott soon learned — maybe in the nick of time — that one of the most valuable roles of our strategic planning process was to keep us out of businesses we shouldn't be in. This single benefit alone turned out to be very important for us. As our hotel business grew by leaps and bounds in the late 1970s and 1980s, our cash flow suddenly grew like mad, too. We were faced with the enviable problem of having to find constructive uses for money.

It would have been a breeze to throw cash at lots of different businesses. Many companies have gotten themselves into trouble that way — acquiring for the sake of acquiring, launching new enterprises simply because they've got the money in hand to give them a whirl. Before we established our formal strategic planning process, we were guilty of the same giddiness. Fortunately, Marriott's new group of planners could sort out our options and supply us with excellent reasons not to get into certain businesses.

That being said, we didn't suddenly stop diversifying in 1980 just because we got our planning act together. If that had been the case, we would have done little more than churn out full-service hotels while keeping our restaurant and airline catering divisions humming along. We did not sit still; we simply became more methodical about analyzing what we got into. Nor did the planners suddenly take control and call the shots. Then as now, major decisions still draw on intuition and experience, not merely numbers.

Some of what we chose to do in the 1980s was simply stick to our knitting. We took a closer look at close-to-home opportunities that fit with what we knew. On the contract services side of our business (restaurants, food service, etc.) — a full one-half of the company — the decade brought major change, much of it in terms of scale. Among other things, we lit a fire under our distribution services and turned what had been mostly an internal supply function into a major growth business (one that we have since exited in order to focus on lodging).

We also plowed our energies into growing our contract food services management operation. My father launched the division in the late 1930s when he began catering meals at the U.S. Treasury building in downtown Washington. Over the years, the business had grown in terms of clients, locations, and numbers of customers served, but we had not really focused on it to the degree that we could have.

Our new strategic planning mindset in the 1980s helped us hone in on the potential to grow the business. Three key acquisitions (Gladieux, Saga, and Service Systems) during the decade transformed us into one of the biggest players in the industry. By 1989, we had expanded the business more than tenfold in just five years, with accounts in places as close to home as the Lockheed Martin corporate cafeteria in Bethesda, Md., and as far-flung as the oil rigs on Alaska's North Slope.

We didn't stop there. Next, we built on 60 years of experience in managing clients' cafeterias and dining rooms to expand our portfolio to include a whole range of facilities management services. Marriott Management Services (MMS) provided not only food service but also plant operation, laundry, housekeeping and energy management to hundreds of clients in business, health care, education and other sectors.

The late 1980s brought other pivotal decisions on the nonlodging side of the company. Specifically, our longest-lived divisions: airline catering and restaurants. After six decades, we knew a lot about both businesses. And because we knew them so intimately, we came to the difficult, but correct, conclusion in 1989 that both had run their courses for us.

From the standpoint of the balance sheet, the decision to put our restaurants and In-Flite on the block was easy. From the standpoint of the company's corporate culture, it was anything but. Marriott's can-do attitude had been born in the hustle of restaurant life during the Great Depression.

A decision to exit our original businesses seemed to cut at the very roots of the company. The competition in the restaurant business was fierce, with the largest chain competitors benefiting from the enormous marketing spend. As a well-run but regional player, we knew we no longer had a competitive advantage in the business. We also recognized the dangers of allowing the status quo to win out over change at the expense of progress.

The decision reflected something else: my own 30-year passion for lodging. My dad had loved the restaurant business, but I loved hotels. Planning them. Building them. Seeing them fill up with people. Some of that passion no doubt reflected the fact that I had gotten in on the ground floor, so to speak, of our hotel business when we opened the doors of Twin Bridges in 1957. Just as my father had cut his teeth on restaurants, I had cut mine on lodging.

While exiting several of our businesses in the 1980s, the lodging half of Marriott underwent the first of a long series of exciting changes. In 1981 we decided to move into other market tiers in the hotel industry. Moderate-priced entry Courtyard by Marriott was the first fruit of that strategic decision to "embrace change."

What's the big deal about a hotel company going into the hotel business?

For Marriott, Courtyard was a very big deal. We had defined ourselves for a quarter of a century as a full-service hotel company. We were known for our expertise in building big boxes loaded with lots of bells and whistles. And we liked being known for our big boxes. Little boxes were what other companies did.

Given how entrenched that attitude was within our corporate culture, it's perhaps a little amazing that Courtyard happened at all. The fact that it did happen is a tribute to two things: one, the dedicated people who worked their fingers to the bone to pull it off, and two, the company's maturity as a manager of change. At the time, Courtyard was a severe test of our organizational ability to foster innovation at the risk of our cherished core identity.

Courtyard disturbed our status quo because it was a clear case of messing with success. Our other diversification efforts — cruise ships, the travel agency, theme parks, home security — had all been sidelines. In those cases, if we didn't make a stellar showing, or if we failed, the damage to our reputation as a hotelier was minimal. Courtyard, on the other hand, had the power to strike right at the heart of the organization. If we blew it, so the arguments ran, we'd lose more than just our investment in Courtyard. We risked 25 years of hard work establishing our name in the industry.

The point was a valid one, but not the only one. Balancing the worries about rocking the boat were a couple of very compelling arguments. One was our perennial urge to grow. Tackling other segments of the lodging market would open up vast new territory for increasing our bottom line. The domestic market could only support a certain number of full-service Marriott hotels. (We were still U.S.-focused at the time.)

The second point was the fact that the idea for Courtyard came straight out of our new strategic planning function. Unlike our earlier diversification efforts, we could bring to bear on Courtyard from conception to completion the kind of discipline and study that would minimize risk and maximize potential. Courtyard was the perfect opportunity to take our new planning function for a serious spin.

The arguments in favor of change won out. For three years, Courtyard incubated in almost complete secrecy. Those who were involved in its planning went into overdrive putting together focus groups, competitor profiles, mock room layouts and just about anything and everything that would help to make Courtyard a textbook case of product planning. The hard work paid off. When our small-size, medium-priced, high-style Courtyard by Marriott was finally unveiled in 1983, it quickly took off.

Part of Courtyard's successful debut was a reflection of the state of the market. The moderate-priced lodging segment had been in need of a fresh product for some time. But it was also the happy culmination of a thousand battles, big and small, that had raged inside Marriott for three years between the forces of fear and confidence, the known and unknown, order and change.

Of the myriad issues we wrestled with, naming the product was one of the most interesting and revealing. Choosing "Courtyard" was easy; a survey of customer preference settled the question. The hard part was deciding whether or not to include the word "Marriott" in the name. Skeptics and worriers expressed concern that attaching the Marriott tag to a moderate-priced product would tarnish the full-service brand name. Courtyard devotees argued that the Marriott name was vital to boost the product's profile and enhance its chances of success.

Was this a case of silly semantics or was it a pivotal point in our history? To my mind, it was very much the latter. By adding "by Marriott" to the Courtyard brand, our organization crossed a philosophical line. We demonstrated a willingness to throw the weight of the company's hard-earned reputation behind an innovation that promised — one way or the other, for good or ill — to redefine the core of Marriott.

The confidence and momentum generated by Courtyard's success in the marketplace quickly led us to the next logical step: diversification into almost every segment of the lodging industry. In 1984, we announced plans for Marriott Suites®; two years later, we unveiled another entry, economy-priced Fairfield Inn by Marriott. Extended-stay brand Residence Inn was acquired in 1987 and tagged with the Marriott name. Other brands followed, including Gaylord Hotels, which we just added in 2012. We're up to 18 brands and still growing.

———

For the first 40 years of our lodging division's existence, Marriott marketed our hotels as a dependable stay. When you booked into a Marriott, you knew exactly what to expect. That was what travelers of the day wanted: consistency. When we introduced our various economy and mid-tier brands in the 1980s and 1990s, guests could choose with confidence among levels of amenities and "frills" based on the brand.

There are still plenty of travelers for whom comfortable familiarity is an important factor in their choice of hotel. But for many, the ambiance of the place where they lay their head at night is becoming every bit as important as the destination itself. Those travelers have represented a new and exciting challenge to us.

Some are looking for classic luxury — a beautifully appointed room and public spaces, plus all the trimmings: championship golf courses, spa treatments, private pristine beaches, an array of dining choices and all the small but important touches that say "deluxe" in any language.

We were in the luxury market in a small way after purchasing the beautiful Camelback Inn® in Scottsdale, Ariz., in 1967. (We added a gorgeous spa to the resort in 1989.) For many years, Camelback was our only truly high-end property. Then, in 1995, we made an acquisition that I consider one of our most important: The Ritz-Carlton, an iconic brand whose name is synonymous with elegance. The purchase of The Ritz-Carlton was one of the quickest decisions we've ever made. And one of the most transformational for us. It established us immediately in the luxury-level marketplace.

In 2001, we formally launched our Luxury Group tier. We transformed our JW Marriott brand (which had started life as a single hotel in downtown D.C.) into a high-end concept that specializes in what we call "quiet luxury" — upscale but unpretentious. In 2002, we opened the luxurious JW Marriott Desert Ridge Resort & Spa, near Phoenix. In just three years, the number of high-end JW Marriott properties tripled, from 10 to 30.

The first BVLGARI® Hotels & Resorts property opened in Milan, Italy, in 2004, a brand to which we later added properties in London, England, and Bali, Indonesia.

Our luxury properties have proven to be a big hit around the world. In fact, we can't build The Ritz-Carlton hotels fast enough in China — it's a brand they've fallen for head over heels. Today we have more than 80 Ritz-Carlton hotels, more than 50 JW Marriott locations and three BVLGARI properties, plus more of each in our pipeline.

Appealing as classic luxury is, there's a growing audience for a different kind of high-end hotel — one that is less traditional. Luxury *and* uniqueness are highly valued by this relatively new crowd of globe-trotting consumers. They don't want to just see the world; they want to *experience* it.

I don't mind confessing that Marriott missed the boat in discovering this market niche on our own. So did most of our competitors. We had all been so busy building out the moderate, business and classic luxury segments that we missed spotting the market's appetite for "lifestyle" hotels and resorts that offer qualities and experiences that are one of a kind.

To give you an idea of how focused we were, it took us a while to wake up fully to the fact that we already had a lifestyle brand right under our nose: Renaissance. We had acquired the Renaissance portfolio in 1997 mainly for its global footprint, not because the brand's unique hotels would appeal to this new kind of traveler. Once we recognized what we had to offer, we got busy giving the brand all the support it needed to reach out to the right consumers. Today we have more than 150 distinctive hotels bearing the Renaissance flag.

Unlike Renaissance, our EDITION brand, which I've mentioned, was a bottom-up effort. It represented the biggest change to Marriott's order since Courtyard in 1983 and The Ritz-Carlton in 1995. Studio 54 creator Ian Schrager had launched the boutique hotel concept in 1984 with the opening of Morgans Hotel in New York City. The Royalton Hotel and Paramount Hotel followed, both of which pioneered the transformation of traditionally quiet hotel lobby space into a hub of social activity. The bar scene at his hotels was fabulous, the restaurants equally so. Ian's unconventional approach to space and design won a following among young, hip urbanites.

When we started thinking about how to enhance our position in the lifestyle tier, Ian came readily to mind. At the time, Marriott didn't have the kind of creative "think outside the box" talent that was needed to do it right. I flew to New York to see the Gramercy Park Hotel, which he had just finished. He got wind that I was coming and so he met me at the hotel to give me a tour. Arne Sorenson did a lot of the follow-up —

he was probably the one keenest on the idea of our getting into the lifestyle space in a big way.

In June 2007, Ian and I jointly announced our partnership and our plans to build as many as 100 EDITION hotels together. *The Wall Street Journal* and others described us as "strange bedfellows," but the industry and media were thoroughly intrigued by the combination of Ian's design aesthetic and our operating expertise. Unfortunately, the recession began not long after, so rollout has been slower than ideal, but we're making progress. In January 2012, we announced five new EDITION hotels, including Manhattan's iconic Clock Tower.

In the meantime, we unveiled our Autograph Collection and AC Hotels by Marriott brands. Both provided terrific answers to the question of how to continue expanding our global reach during an economic downturn. Properties in our Autograph Collection are independent hotels like the iconic Casa Monica Hotel in St. Augustine, Fla., and The Cosmopolitan™, a gorgeous luxury hotel on the Strip in Las Vegas. Autograph hotels benefit from access to Marriott's global marketing platform, and we're able to offer our guests more choices of unique destinations. Our Marriott Rewards customers earn points for stays at any of the Autograph hotels.

Our AC Hotels by Marriott brand is a joint venture with our partner AC Hotels, an award-winning Spanish hotel group. The venture has extended Marriott's reach into dozens of beautiful destinations in Europe at a time when we're aiming to double our presence there. The four-star hotels in the portfolio are urban, moderately priced and contemporary in flavor. Guests can stay at any of about 90 AC Hotels by Marriott in cities across France, Spain, Italy and Portugal.

Combined with our global expansion, the addition of so many appealing and diverse brands to our portfolio is the most visible change in our company in the past three decades. Another exciting change has been the transformation of our approach to strategic planning. Instead of the stand-alone department that we depended on for years, planning today takes a dynamic and fluid form. We eagerly pull together talent from every relevant area of the company to brainstorm about the future — in essence, we now crowdsource the very best ideas and insights that our entire global team has to offer.

A great example is a two-day meeting we facilitated in August 2011 at the Washington Marriott Wardman Park Hotel in D.C. Our Marriott Hotels & Resorts brand leaders invited 50 people representing all disciplines and parts of the globe to unleash their imaginations on the challenge of giving our 50-year-old signature brand a fresh and bold vision for the future. Leaders from brand, sales, marketing, operations and communications and the team from Insights, Strategy and Innovation attended. An innovation consulting firm from the United Kingdom — eatbigfish — led the group through two days of guided exercises and brainstorming. By the time the group was finished, the meeting room walls were filled with flip charts and thousands of Post-it Notes® and sticky dots that indicated bold ideas and priorities for how Marriott could evolve to "host the new world brilliantly."

While eatbigfish helped us define what it terms our "lighthouse identity," the ideas and core beliefs about the Marriott brand came straight from our own team, the people best equipped to define the future strategy for our brands.

I'm thrilled that we've embraced this new inclusive approach to strategic planning. I think it's going to be a critical competency for any company that wants to remain relevant to its customers. My dad used to say, "Success is never final." Today's spin might be "Innovation is never final." Companies that don't think boldly will inevitably find themselves falling behind those that do. You can lead change, or it can lead you. The trick is to manage risk productively.

———

Talking about risk reminds me of a day almost 30 years ago when I had to make a major decision that promised to affect the company for years to come. To appreciate the story, you have to understand that my father was a devoted fan of AstroTurf®. He loved the fresh, green color and the texture, and wanted us to use it every chance we could, to cover bare concrete sidewalks, swimming pool decks, room balconies and virtually anything else that didn't move. Dad was constantly after me to use large quantities. He even checked AstroTurf prices on a near-weekly basis at the country hardware store not far from the family farm in Virginia. He would walk into the office on Monday morning, quote the latest price and wait expectantly for me to jump at the chance to buy in bulk at the store's low rate, which was about half our procurement price. If we bought it in the country, he pointed out, we could use twice as much.

The AstroTurf update became a predictable part of our weekly ritual. But it wasn't until May 1982 that I really appreciated its true value. That month, I was confronted with the task of making the biggest financial decision of my career. For several months, we had been working feverishly to finalize development plans for a new hotel in Times Square at Broadway and 45th Street in New York City. I had to decide whether to commit Marriott to build a large $500 million hotel in a run-down, seedy area that might or might not come back to life. It was a huge risk. On the afternoon of the final day that we had to make up our minds, I was in my office mulling over last-minute details of the deal. The phone rang. The landowner in New York City was calling to remind me that this was the last day of our option. If we didn't buy the land by the end of the day, the price would go up. Before I could take his call, another telephone line lit up. This one was the general contractor reporting that he could not get a "no-strike" clause accepted in the construction contract. Did we want to take a strike risk? Just then another light on my telephone lit up. The New York City mayor's office was calling to get confirmation of our decision to go forward (they hoped), so the project could be announced at a big press conference. Last, but not least, the fourth light came on. My father was on the line. My assistant wanted to know who I wanted to talk to first.

I took my father's call. In an angry voice, he demanded, "When are you going to put AstroTurf on the balconies of the Twin Bridges hotel?"

Just when I might have been most dismayed to have to listen to yet another lecture on the merits of AstroTurf, I was, in fact, relieved. My father's simple question about fake grass brought me back to down earth. His call turned out to be just what I needed to take a deep breath and put the biggest deal of my life into proper perspective.

My decision about whether or not to take the $500 million risk? The 1,900-room Marriott Marquis opened in 1985, becoming the anchor that helped revitalize Times Square. But not before I made sure my dad got all the AstroTurf his heart desired.

———

PART IV:
ACT WITH INTEGRITY

"Watch your thoughts, for they become words.
Choose your words, for they become actions.
Understand your actions, for they become habits.
Study your habits, for they will become your character.
Develop your character, for it becomes your destiny."

— OLIVER WENDELL HOLMES
writer

CHAPTER 9:
CHECK YOUR EGO
AT THE DOOR

CHAPTER 10:
LISTEN TO YOUR HEART —
AND DON'T WASTE TIME ON REGRET

9

CHECK YOUR EGO
AT THE DOOR

"You shouldn't gloat about anything you've done;
you ought to keep going and find something better to do."

— DAVID PACKARD, cofounder, Hewlett-Packard

n 1932, the year I was born, the United States was deeply
mired in the Great Depression. Unemployment hit almost
25 percent that year. More than 13 million Americans had
lost their jobs in the prior three years. Ten thousand banks
had failed since 1929.

Although I barely remember the Depression, I've been
around long enough to have lived through subsequent economic
downturns — seven, to be exact — including the most recent
one that began in 2008. Even so, I was astonished when the
venerable financial firm Lehman Brothers filed for Chapter
11 bankruptcy protection on September 15, 2008. The filing
kicked off the largest bankruptcy in U.S. history; Lehman
held $600 billion in assets. It also fueled fears of another Great
Depression.

As things continued to unravel that autumn, we saw other
icons of the financial world brought to the brink of ruin, at a
speed that was unsettling to witness. Some of the self-immolation
stemmed from a systemic arrogance that blinded those companies

to their own vulnerability. The current crop of leaders at some of our biggest banks and brokerages considered themselves invincible. They learned otherwise.

The debacle of 2008 reminded me of a time 20 years earlier when Marriott also forgot the simple rule that what goes up, especially in the marketplace, can come crashing down. We didn't have $600 billion at stake, but it was nonetheless a profoundly humbling experience and one that I hope we'll never forget.

My first inkling that something was amiss came around late 1988, when I attended a big awards banquet at our Camelback Inn in Scottsdale, Ariz. The purpose of the evening was to honor the real estate developers who had secured the greatest number of sites for new Courtyard, Fairfield Inn, and Residence Inn hotels during the previous 12 months. At the time, we were opening about 100 hotels annually and had plenty of others in various stages of design and construction. Our development pipeline was going full steam, in large part due to the work of the people we were honoring.

The evening was a perfect symbol of the fast-paced, no-holds-barred days of American business in the 1980s. Deal making had been raised to an art during the decade, and deal makers had become the new stars, capturing daily headlines with the scale and scope of their financial wizardry (think Donald Trump). Billions of dollars were spent and made on friendly mergers and not-so-friendly acquisitions across every sector.

In the lodging industry, the atmosphere and pace of expansion had likewise become supercharged, fueled in part by new provisions in the federal tax code that encouraged individuals to invest in real estate. Approximately 1 million rooms were added to the U.S. lodging system during the 1980s, the rate of growth accelerating as the decade wore on. There seemed to be a hotel being built on every corner.

As I watched the awards being handed out that night,

I thought about the market explosion that had led all of us to that banquet room. I realized that I wasn't entirely comfortable with what I was seeing and hearing. But everyone else in the room seemed to be so bullish and positive about our business that I set my worry aside and joined in the celebration. After all, all signs at the time were positive. Our hotels were filling up as fast as they could be finished, and capital was plentiful. Why not just keep going?

Then suddenly — *wham!* — in 1990, the wave of hotel expansion that Marriott had been riding crashed. The causes will sound all too familiar: an abrupt tailspin of the U.S. real estate market, rising tensions in the Middle East and a recession, among other things.

These factors alone would have been challenging enough on their own, but when combined with a failure on my part to act on my gut-level concerns about overbuilding, they spelled disaster. When the Japanese withdrew as large-scale investors in American real estate after Japan's Nikkei index nosedived between January and October 1990, it was the final straw.

The price we paid when things went sour was dramatic. We took a stiff hit on our stock price, had to lay off two departments of hard-working people, endured a brief takeover scare and—like Apple a few years later—had the dubious pleasure of reading premature Marriott epitaphs in the business media. It was not fun.

We faced another big problem: a backlog of lodging properties that our development team had been dutifully churning out before the real estate market went south.

As long as we had been able to sell hotels quickly — never a problem in the 1980s — our develop-build-sell-and-manage strategy had worked like a charm. Now faced with no buyers for our hotels, no new projects were started, and we suddenly had more than $1.5 billion invested in unsold property sitting on our books. The start of the first Gulf War in 1991 further added to the financial pain as people grew cautious about airline travel.

No one was more angst-ridden about our financial dilemma than I. After years of listening to my father's heartfelt lectures on the evils of debt, I felt as if I had single-handedly let him and the company down by allowing us to get so caught up in the gross overbuilding of the business. My dad had passed away in 1985 and wasn't alive to see the drama unfold. Even so, I could almost hear him chiding me from on high, "Don't say I didn't warn you."

Our biggest problem was our debt level, which reached $3.6 billion at year-end 1990. Development isn't cheap. But we were determined not to follow the path our competitors took: sell good sites and hotels at fire-sale prices. In spite of the fevered pace at which we had snapped up locations in the 1980s for our new hotels, our selections by and large had been solid choices, not junk. When the real estate market perked up again, we knew we would be glad we had not let those prime sites go for a song.

Simply sitting on our hands and waiting for the market to come around again wasn't an option, though. For better or worse, I'm an impatient man. I'll take action over treading water any day. The real estate crash had kicked up opportunities that we couldn't ignore. Many competitors' lodging properties were in the hands of banks, the federal Resolution Trust Corporation and other institutions that knew nothing about hotel management and didn't want to learn. Opportunities abounded for Marriott to pick up management contracts. But to do so, we needed to have our own house in order.

In January 1992, company veteran Bill Shaw took over as president of the Marriott Service Group, the nonlodging half of the business. (We hadn't yet divested ourselves of our food and distribution businesses.) Bill had spent the previous two years in the role of chief financial officer, shepherding us through the worst of our cash-flow problems. To fill the empty slot left by Bill's promotion, we hired Steve Bollenbach. Steve was just finishing up a long-term assignment helping Donald Trump restructure his finances. (We weren't the only ones with money challenges.)

Steve had been Marriott's treasurer for several years in the early 1980s. So he had the advantage of looking at our debt problem from the unique vantage point of a two-time insider and recent outsider. After studying us for a few months, he came up with an idea both natural and radical: Why not split the company in two?

The concept of splitting Marriott into two pieces was natural in the sense that spinoffs were coming into vogue in the early 1990s. Many companies were slimming down in an effort to refocus on their core businesses; others wanted to get a fresh start after being hammered by the recession. We wanted to do both.

The split Steve had in mind was radical. His idea was to allow the original 65-year-old Marriott Corporation (soon renamed Host Marriott) to keep the real estate — including the debt associated with it — and spin off our hotel management business into a new company. The new Marriott International would be virtually debt-free, giving it more flexibility to go after management contracts and get the blood moving again throughout the Marriott enterprise.

The two companies would maintain separate boards of directors, hold separate annual meetings and operate separately. Marriott International would manage Host Marriott's properties under long-term agreements.

In one decisive move, Marriott took care of both of its most important immediate goals. Our real estate investments would be managed by one company, while our hotel management and franchising skills could be marketed aggressively by the other company.

Important as the plan's practical aspects were, there was another dimension to the split that reached more deeply into the heart of our problems. Splitting the company into two separate entities would fix something fundamental that had gone askew during the heady days just before the 1990 crash. In the aggressive atmosphere of the 1980s, we had let ourselves get pulled too far away from who we really were. Steve's plan would get us back to our core identity. Marriott was (and is) not about debt, real estate ownership and deals. We're about management and service.

Marriott still facilitates hotel deals, of course. But our competitive advantage is developing and growing our brands, taking care of customers and managing and franchising hotels, not just moving assets around on a balance sheet. Where Marriott had gone off track in the 1980s was in letting development drive the organization rather than support it. In the change/order dynamic, Marriott had lost the critical balance between the two. Sometimes it takes an old friend who knows you well and has seen you in good moments and bad to remind you of who you really are. Steve was that friend.

When the split was announced in October 1992, I was prepared for the novelty of the plan to raise some eyebrows. I was not ready for an intensely negative reaction in certain quarters. When the near-term value of our public bonds declined, we were charged with acting in bad faith toward our bondholders.

The criticism stung. While Marriott has never been a pushover, we're not a bully either. We value our reputation as a "white hat" kind of company — one that places great stock in its integrity. I honestly didn't think the charge against us was well-founded. Steve and our legal department (headed by Sterling Colton, our general counsel and son of my father's original partner, Hugh Colton) had been fastidious about crafting the plan for the split to adhere to the law and ensuring that Host would be able to pay its obligation. Even so, we had to face inevitable lawsuits. Fortunately the cases were eventually settled to all parties' satisfaction.

The criticism and the court cases taught me that even the best intentions can be misinterpreted. How you choose to respond to the misinterpretation is critical. Stick to your guns, by all means, if you're sure you've done nothing wrong, but do so honorably and in a way that reflects your principles.

In the midst of the legal fireworks, I remained convinced that the decision to split was the correct choice. Our shareholders agreed, voting at our annual meeting in July 1993 to accept the plan by an 85 percent margin. Three months later, the two companies became official. Just two years after that, Host Marriott split into Host Marriott (now named Host Hotels & Resorts) and Host Marriott Services. The reasoning again was to enhance the ability of the two entities to distinguish missions and goals.

Since that time, we've had to navigate not only the challenging years following 9/11, but also two wars in the Middle East, major jumps in oil prices and the Wall Street meltdown. Dire headlines prompted major cases of the jitters, not only for Marriott but also for many of our customers, our vendors and our partners. The travel industry as a whole felt the pain beginning in the summer of 2001 — even before 9/11 happened — and continued to feel it on and off through 2010. We were fortunate to enjoy great years from 2005 to 2007.

One important thing Marriott did throughout that up-and-down period was strike a balance between being realistic about the challenges we faced and being optimistic about the future.

We moved forward with our long-term plans to expand globally, but at a rate that didn't pretend that we would somehow magically be immune to the forces of geopolitics, economics and warfare.

Compare that mindset to our attitude in the late 1980s when one of our senior executives stood in front of colleagues at a hotel industry conference and stated flatly "Marriott is so powerful we can build through any cycle." I wince when I think how arrogant we surely sounded. And what a lesson in humility we learned shortly thereafter.

———————

Our timeshare business was also hurt by the 2008 recession. Demand declined, loan defaults increased and the loan securitization market shut down, reducing our access to capital for the business. This was somewhat surprising because the business had weathered past recessions easily. What was the difference this time? The economic meltdown was one big difference as investors feared lending and customers feared borrowing. Another difference was the amount of inventory tied up in our new luxury fractional products that fell in value as the luxury residential real estate market collapsed. Having said that, the business performed far better than others in its industry. Strong brands, a reputation for quality and strong owner satisfaction made a big difference in weathering this storm.

Marriott had grown its timeshare business to be enormous. By 2010, we had 60 timeshare properties and 400,000 owner families. But in the eyes of Wall Street, it looked like an increasingly odd fit with parent company Marriott, which had slowly shed its other businesses to become largely a hotel management and franchise company. It was also very capital intensive and was large enough to do very well on its own. So in 2011, we turned once again to the spinoff concept.

After a lot of internal discussion in October 2011, Marriott's board of directors approved a plan to spinoff Marriott Vacation Club® International into a separate entity, Marriott Vacations Worldwide℠ Corporation. The company would retain the use of Marriott brands, paying a royalty fee to Marriott International (MVCI). Because MVCI had held its own during the worst of the real estate shakeout, we felt confident that it would do just fine without being aboard the corporate mother ship.

Like other changes we've weathered, the MVCI spinoff had its good and bad points. On one hand, it was tough to let go of a 27-year-old business we'd built from scratch and that had proved its mettle. The upside was that the separation would allow both companies to focus exclusively on their core businesses. I'm delighted that the stocks of both companies have performed well on Wall Street since the split.

How we prepared for the spinoff was very important to us. We wanted to be sure that all our stakeholders were included — from shareholders and lenders to timeshare owners and MVCI associates, many of whom had migrated from the lodging part of the business. We held town hall meetings to discuss the split and then hosted a celebration when it was completed on November 21, 2011. As we bid farewell to MVCI, I couldn't help but contrast everybody's celebratory mood to the tearful good-byes we witnessed when employees were forced to leave Bear Stearns after its meltdown in March 2008.

———

When dangerous cracks began to show in the nation's subprime mortgage market in 2007, I was reminded of what Marriott had weathered in the early 1990s and, to a lesser degree, after 9/11. As it became clear that the U.S. economy — and possibly the global economy, too — was in danger of being brought down by the hubris of a relative few, I could only shake my head. The leadership of the nation's major financial institutions had gotten so caught up in the fever of moneymaking that any semblance of caution — not to mention integrity — had been tossed to the winds.

Worse, simply because of the nature of their business, the most troubled finance houses had the power to take down other companies and endanger the financial security of millions of average Americans. In the five years since the economic crisis began, hundreds of books, articles, blogs and documentaries have dissected why things went so horribly wrong. Many touch on what I consider the central issue: the lack of a healthy institutional culture to keep hubris and questionable judgment in check. Whether by acts of omission or of commission, the financial companies' leadership failed to instill a sense of humility among employees that might have gone a long way to temper the actions of those most to blame for the economic meltdown.

For companies that disappeared during the crisis — like Lehman Brothers and Bear Stearns — it's too late to fix their broken cultures. But for those that survived the ordeal, I hope they're working around the clock to reorder their priorities.

One of the best things the financial sector could do for itself is keep on board some of its key employees from the meltdown period. Not the ones who had a direct hand in creating the crisis, of course, but others who weathered the storm and learned from it. I consider it a blessing that Marriott is staffed today by associates who lived through some of our most challenging days with us. Their experience and memories of the tough times are our best hedge against believing that it can't happen again.

10

LISTEN TO YOUR HEART –
AND DON'T WASTE TIME ON REGRET

"Care more than others think wise.
Risk more than others think safe.
Dream more than others think practical.
Expect more than others think possible."

— HOWARD SCHULTZ, CEO, Starbucks Coffee Company

In 1965, Marriott opened its fifth hotel, a 500-room convention facility two blocks east of Peachtree Street in downtown Atlanta, Ga. We poured everything we had into creating a showcase property that would put Marriott on the map. As we were putting on the finishing touches, we learned that a hotel under construction nearby was up for sale. At the invitation of the architect and developer John Portman, a team of Marriott hotel people toured the site.

Our guys shook their heads over the layout of the heart of the house. They craned their necks and squinted to find the tip-top of an open-air, multistory space in the central lobby that wasted thousands of cubic feet. They exchanged glances over the location of restaurants and ballrooms. Other aspects of the unusual design came in for silent censure as well.

"It's a disaster! The building will never work. We'd have to be crazy to buy it," was the group's considered opinion. Besides, who in his right mind would want to have two hotels of the same brand in one city?

We politely declined to make an offer.

Out of our "wisdom" was born the Hyatt hotel chain.

As soon as the Hyatt Regency® Atlanta threw open its doors, a steady stream of people passed through the hotel simply to stand in the "Awesome!" spot in the lobby — the best vantage point for taking in the dizzying height of the light-filled atrium. In no time, almost every major city decided it needed to have a similar showplace hotel. Hyatt Regency hotels soon sprouted up in key markets around the country. All because we couldn't see past the building's unusual mechanics to the architect's grander vision.

It's now laughably naive to think that having two Marriott hotels in the same city was a crazy idea. Today, we have dozens of hotels in the Atlanta area.

The Hyatt Regency Atlanta story is a perfect example of the thousands of forks in the road that Marriott has faced over the years. Most forks have been small decisions that simply keep the daily grind grinding along. But once in a while, we face a choice that turns out to have dramatic ramifications. As we learned in Atlanta almost 50 years ago, you can't always tell which decisions will reverberate longest until well after your choice has been made. All you can do is make the best decision possible at that moment, be totally honest with yourself about the pros and cons and then cross your fingers and get moving.

Making decisions is a big part of running a business. Not a day goes by in the life of a company that you don't commit yourself to a particular path, turning down one or more opportunities in favor of another. A few simple rules keep me from getting bogged down by the dozens of puzzles, queries and opportunities that land on my desk every day.

First, be willing to make a decision. Don't just kick the can down the road. Not everybody finds this easy. My father hated making decisions, for fear that some better option was just around the corner or the risk was too great.

I don't suffer from the same kind of indecisiveness that plagued my dad. In fact, I'm sometimes accused — with some justification — of being very impatient about making decisions. I'd rather make a decision and get on with it. If *significant* new information comes in, I'm willing to listen and adjust accordingly.

The second rule for decision making is to do your homework. Remember our travel agency and home security businesses? Our organizational decision-making skills improved markedly after we put more muscle into disciplined study. I don't think we would have been able to diversify successfully into the limited-service lodging market, for example, had we not devoted so much energy to studying the competition thoroughly in order to design Courtyard by Marriott.

On the flip side, study needs to come to an end at some point and a choice must be made. Don't let dotting *i*'s and crossing *t*'s become a convenient way to avoid making a decision. If you suffer from analysis paralysis, you know what I'm talking about. More often than not, the critical information needed to make an *informed* but not necessarily *perfect* decision does not require delving into microscopic details.

Our decisions to exit Marriott Management Services®, Marriott Distribution Services®, ExecuStay® and Marriott Senior Living Services®; to spin off MVCI; and to focus on the booming lodging markets of China, India, and Brazil (among others) are good examples of doing our homework, making decisions and implementing them without second-guessing ourselves into a dither.

Another great example is our decision to expand into the "lifestyle hotel" market. Our decision didn't come after years of agonized debate. It came after we watched the "boutique" hotel market grow past the point of being just a tiny niche. If we didn't want to be left behind, we (and the rest of the hotel industry) needed to develop our own fresh products to compete in that space.

How we went about it — by inventing EDITION, Autograph Collection and AC Hotels by Marriott and reinvigorating our Renaissance brand — required additional time and realistic planning. But the basic decision about whether or not to move into that market was made with dispatch after we realized that a worthy competitor had developed more than a passing trend.

Of course, homework only gets you so far. Research and analysis should give you the hard data you need to debate a decision with intelligence and insight, but facts alone aren't always enough to make a correct decision.

Which brings me to my third rule of decision making: Listen to your heart.

Factoring your heart into a decision is not the same as winging it. And it's not a convenient cover for indulging wishful thinking. It is experience speaking. Nothing — not even number crunching at its best — can take the place of cumulative knowledge. The central ingredients of heart are your understanding of your business, and the internal compass that develops after years of experience.

I'll give you two examples to illustrate my point. One decision was made virtually overnight. Another involved more than two years of careful study. In the end, heart — not numbers — was the true deciding factor in each case.

In February 1995, Jim Sullivan, our former head development executive, was meeting with Fred Malek, former head of Marriott's Lodging Group, for one of the pair's periodic "What's up with you?" chats. As Jim was heading out the door at the end, Fred casually asked, "Oh, by the way, you wouldn't be interested in The Ritz-Carlton, would you?" Jim quickly closed the door and sat back down, and on April 25, less than three months later, Marriott and The Ritz-Carlton closed a deal to bring The Ritz-Carlton into the Marriott family.

The determination to acquire a major interest in the

management of The Ritz-Carlton's 31 hotels was probably the quickest major decision that we have ever made. We had been thinking about getting into the luxury tier of lodging, so the opportunity was right up our alley. We know the hotel business, we were very familiar with The Ritz-Carlton product and its great market appeal, and we could see clearly that the fit would be a good one. The number crunching and due diligence before the paperwork was signed was important, but it was definitely not the deciding factor. Heart was. We just knew it was the right choice.

The second example of heart in action involved a two-year debate in the early 1980s over whether or not Marriott should acquire Disney®. Our flirtation with the idea is probably the company's most dramatic example of a well-studied fork in the road. One former Marriott executive who was a pivotal figure in exploring the Disney possibility believes it's one of the most significant "roads not taken" in American business history.

His characterization is too grand, but Disney definitely ranks as a defining moment for Marriott. And not for the first time: In 1957, my father turned down the chance to buy the hotel at Disneyland®.

When we began studying Disney, creator Walt Disney's original empire had been treading water for a number of years. Walt had died in 1966, and many observers felt that the creative spark of the company had died with him. The Disney organization was ripe for revitalization.

I was attracted to the idea of acquiring Disney because of the company's legendary success with Disneyland and Disney World® and, naturally, the hotels associated with the parks. The combination of the Marriott and Disney brands seemed like a phenomenal marriage. Both organizations are family oriented and share clean-cut values. Each had charismatic founders who forged strong corporate cultures. Together, we might have dominated the family and leisure travel markets.

The idea of acquiring Disney had plenty to recommend it, but — unlike The Ritz-Carlton — it was not a decision that could be made in the blink of an eye. For one thing, Disney was larger than Marriott. We'd have had to borrow $2.5 billion to bankroll the acquisition. Even in the high-rolling days of the 1980s, that kind of money would have been a bet-the-ranch transaction for our company. Disney consisted of more than hotels; we would be taking on the crème de la crème of theme parks, plus a film business about which we knew absolutely nothing. And there was a good chance that Disney wasn't going to welcome our interest.

We quietly studied Disney, trying to get a feel for not only the numbers but also the culture and traditions of the company. The Disney organization was legendary for being tight-lipped about its internal workings. We even approached Disney to do a small hotel deal to get our foot in the door, meet the key players and get some firsthand experience with the company.

For more than two years, we scrutinized Disney — coming as close as I've ever experienced to a case of analysis paralysis on my watch — until we knew the company almost as well as we knew ourselves. In the end, it came down to exactly that: knowing our strengths and weaknesses well enough to have a strong feeling that the acquisition simply was not right for Marriott.

What precisely did my heart tell me? For one thing, too much of Disney's success and intrinsic value rested on a creative spark that I didn't feel we had at the time. I knew that we would not be comfortable trying to run a business — especially one larger than Marriott — that depended on a steady stream of creative juices focused on entertainment to make it work. We had learned this lesson in our own Great America theme parks. I couldn't, at that point in time, foresee finding anyone to take over Disney and provide it with the imaginative leadership that I knew the company needed to reach its potential. It was too risky to acquire Disney if we couldn't turn it around and make it extremely successful.

At one point, we looked into the possibility of asking someone else to buy Disney's movie division, leaving Marriott with the parks and hotels. Although Disney's film business in the early 1980s was small compared to what it is today, it was one of the key parts of the company that I personally didn't feel comfortable with. We suggested to Coca-Cola that they take a look at the film side; they owned Columbia Pictures Industries Inc., and former baseball commissioner, Fay Vincent, was running it as president and CEO. Marriott's chief financial officer, Gary Wilson, and Vincent talked it over during a flight aboard Coca-Cola's corporate jet. Vincent gave it some thought and made a midair decision: no thanks. Columbia was providing enough challenges at the time, and another film venture didn't sound appealing. Not long after that, I decided to let the opportunity go.

The upshot is that Michael Eisner soon came along and helped catapult Disney back into the forefront of the entertainment business.

Eisner once asked me why I decided not to buy Disney. I told him it was because I didn't know someone like him existed. If I'd been aware that a leader with his creative talent was available to run the show, I might have made a different decision.

The reality is I probably still would have said no. My personal desire to be deeply involved would have prevented me from giving even someone as talented as Eisner the run of the place — which is what would have been required to make the acquisition a success. I would also have worried constantly about Disney's size and complexity siphoning attention away from Marriott's original businesses. I would not have been happy to make that sacrifice.

We made the right decision about Disney based on what we knew and what my heart told me at the time. I won't deny that the high financial stakes were part of the decision — the price tag of Disney would have exceeded Marriott's total annual sales at the time — but ultimately I made the choice based on knowing my own limits. The fact that it took us nearly three years to reach a definitive decision itself tells me that we probably made the correct choice. If Disney had been right for us, it would not have taken us so long to see it.

The Disney question is a fine example of an opportunity that came and went, never to return. It's also a good illustration of what I think is the fourth rule of decision making: Don't waste time regretting, revisiting or ruminating over what might have been. As I mentioned earlier, "deciding to decide" can be liberating.

Have there been moments when I've wondered what might have happened if Marriott had acquired Disney? Sure. But I made peace with the decision years ago. The making peace part is important in decision making. If you spend time going over the what-ifs of every decision you make, you do nothing but waste time that could otherwise be going into exploring new opportunities.

Occasionally, circumstances change so dramatically that it's appropriate to take another look at an opportunity from a fresh perspective. When we turned down the chance to buy John Portman's original Atlanta hotel in 1965, for example, it was the right decision for Marriott at the time. At that stage in Marriott's evolution as a hotel company, we weren't ready to appreciate the cutting-edge architecture of a John Portman. We were still focused on getting those all-important basics in place and opening our first downtown hotel.

Twenty years later, the story was different. By then, we were at a point in our development that having a couple of Portman-designed properties in our portfolio was the right fit and gave us a nice halo. Times Square in New York City was the site of one of the two Marriott Marquis hotels that Portman put together for us. The other is the Marriott Marquis in — yes — Atlanta. There was something especially appropriate about having Atlanta be the site of one of Portman's designs for us.

We haven't only revisited decisions about individual properties. We've also taken another look at broad philosophical issues when the timing has been right. Hotel franchising is the example that comes to mind first. I've already touched on Marriott's earliest — and ambivalent — experiences with hotel franchising. We put franchising on hold after our Marriott Inns franchise program failed to flourish in the 1960s. Among other things, our corporate culture just wasn't ready to embrace the idea of being a franchise organization.

By the early 1990s, when we needed to jump-start growth after a couple of years of treading water, our attitude toward franchising was much more open-minded. We came back to the issue with a different viewpoint, different needs and different goals. Hence, our decision was different.

———

The importance of thinking with our hearts as well as our heads is reflected throughout Marriott's human rights policy, which we formally approved in 2006. One company can't fix all the problems in the world, but we can and *should* address the ones that are right under our noses. Especially when those problems involve how people are treated.

As Marriott develops its business around the world, we believe we have a responsibility to help protect vulnerable children from exploitation in the communities in which we operate. Tourism does not cause the exploitation of children. However, perpetrators sometimes use the tourism infrastructure, such as hotels, in their pursuits. The latest estimates indicate that 1.2 million children are trafficked worldwide each year. We're staunchly opposed to human trafficking and the exploitation of children. We do not recruit child labor, and we're strong advocates for the elimination of such practices.

In 2011, we joined with other industry leaders through the International Tourism Partnership, a nongovernmental organization, to develop and publish a formal industry position on human trafficking. We train our associates to spot and report suspected cases of prostitution and trafficking to the authorities.

Striking a balance between our customers' preferences and our sense of propriety isn't always easy. For years, we've offered adult-content video as part of our pay-per-view entertainment options — a policy that I personally wasn't crazy about but felt compelled to allow to remain competitive. Now that many of our guests use their laptops to access games and movies, I don't feel it's vital to continue to make adult content available through our hotel system. In January 2011, we announced that we'll be phasing it out of our in-room options.

Another area that I have strong personal feelings about is gambling. Beginning in the late 1970s and early 1980s, many lodging chains began to turn their attention to legalized gambling. It's a lucrative business and, in the eyes of some, a glamorous one.

We chose not to follow the pack. The pros and cons of getting into destination gambling (or gaming, as some call it) were pretty straightforward for us. The main argument on the side of entering the business is the power of the established Marriott name. We were virtually assured of success if we opted to build casino hotels.

In my mind, however, the negatives readily outweighed the positives, and still do today. I've watched many Marriott competitors go so far down the road into gambling that their original business — lodging — has become a secondary thought. Their attention has been diverted away from what was once their core business. Given our competitive advantage in lodging, I couldn't see allowing the company to be pulled away from what we do best.

Some would argue that if gambling is lucrative as a business, Marriott as a public company has an obligation to pursue it. I strongly disagree. Corporate leaders all across the country make decisions every day about which businesses to get into or out of. And not all those decisions are based on just economics. Investors must weigh the pros and cons of the gaming business for themselves.

Is our decision about gambling written in stone? No. Like any rule, there are exceptions. Today, we have a half dozen small casinos in Marriott hotels overseas, largely to be competitive in local markets. Here in the United States, if one of our key urban markets legalized gambling and all our competitors leaped in, we'd be forced to at least revisit the decision to remain competitive. But I can guarantee that we would be very careful about how we'd go about it.

PART V:
SERVE OUR WORLD

"We make a living by what we get,
but we make a life by what we give."

— WINSTON CHURCHILL
British Prime Minister

CHAPTER 11:

NOT-SO-RANDOM
ACTS OF KINDNESS

CHAPTER 12:

WHY THE JOURNEY
IS THE REWARD

11

NOT-SO-RANDOM
ACTS OF KINDNESS

===================================

*"It's easy to make a buck. It's a lot tougher
to make a difference."*

— TOM BROKAW, journalist

On January 12, 2010, a catastrophic 7.0 magnitude earthquake leveled part of the Caribbean island nation of Haiti. The devastation was almost beyond imagining. Within minutes, possibly as many as 100,000 people were wiped off the face of the earth. Fathers, mothers, sons, daughters — gone in the blink of an eye.

How do you begin to get your head around such a loss? Hundreds of thousands of the survivors lost their homes, family members and livelihoods. To my mind, the Haiti earthquake ranks as one of the greatest tragedies of our time.

One of the poorest countries in the world, Haiti was totally unprepared to deal with the crisis and its aftermath. While international aid organizations tripped over each other trying to determine where to begin to deal with a disaster of such proportions, refugee camps filled up within days, bringing huge problems in sanitation, disease, housing, food and crime.

Marriott didn't have a hotel in Haiti when the quake happened, but we have plenty of associates from there who work for us at our South Florida properties and also in New York and New Jersey. Our Harbor Beach Marriott Resort & Spa in Florida has almost 300 Haitians on staff. The Haitian associates I've met have always impressed me with their spirit, compassion and love for their home country.

Like many other companies and communities in the days immediately following the quake, we answered the call for supplies and contributions. But it didn't feel like enough — particularly considering how incredibly loyal our Haitian associates are. So we started thinking about what else we could do that would make a difference — a tangible long-term difference — to the island's recovery. Our answer? Develop a Marriott hotel to provide jobs and signal to the world that Haiti is "open for business." In November 2011, President Bill Clinton, who has been Haiti's greatest ally, and Denis O'Brien, CEO of Digicel®, the cellular phone company that will build and own the hotel, joined us in Port-au-Prince to make the announcement. When the Marriott hotel opens there in 2014, we expect to employ as many as 200 Haitians. Our hotel project will have a multiplier effect as we attract investors to Haiti to do business.

I'm highlighting our Haiti effort not to give ourselves a pat on the back, but because it's an initiative that fits hand in glove with our belief that great companies exist for reasons beyond simply making money. Marriott is in the fortunate position of being able to provide employment opportunities and promote foreign investment in a country that is often overlooked. If our presence in Haiti helps to open up possibilities for a ravaged community that needs stability and hope for the future, we're delighted to be of assistance. And, of course, we hope that other companies will take a cue from us and join in the effort if they can.

The poverty of Haiti brings to mind something else that I strongly believe: Happiness doesn't lie in material possessions but in helping and serving others. An "abundant life" — a theme we hear often these days — consists of far more than piling up "stuff" in a race to see who ends up with the most. We all know people whose wealth and possessions don't create happiness, but undermine it.

Many Haitians, of course, are so poor that they won't suffer from material overload anytime soon. They're still lacking many basic necessities, including clean water and roofs over their heads. Yet in spite of their poverty, many Haitians seem to be more resilient, more optimistic and more content than people I've met for whom no amount of wealth will ever be enough.

———

Our initiative in Haiti is one among thousands of gestures that Marriott and our associates have made over the years in an effort to make a difference in the communities in which we work and live. Marriott has been serving people for well over 80 years — long before it was called social responsibility — so it's not surprising that the quality we call our "spirit to serve" spills over beyond the workplace. Most of our associates have an innate desire to be useful to others, or they wouldn't be drawn to our business in the first place. Thanks to our associates' big hearts, we've gotten involved — individually and as a company — in scores of great causes over the years.

I'd like to highlight a few that we've found most fulfilling. Each touches on at least one of five global issues that we as a company have decided to focus on: poverty alleviation, the environment, community workforce development, the well-being of children, and diversity and inclusion. Plenty of other issues merit attention, but these five are the ones where we think we can make an impact. We use the shorthand SERVE® to sum up the mission: **S**helter and food, **E**nvironment, **R**eadiness for hotel careers, **V**itality of children and **E**mbracing global diversity and inclusion.

One of our most inclusive initiatives is our annual Spirit To Serve Our Communities Day, held every May. The program grew out of one-day volunteer efforts that some of our properties had begun organizing on their own. The idea of making it an official event that all Marriott associates could opt into was irresistible. We launched the campaign in the United States in 1999, and today it has expanded to the 70-plus countries where we have hotels.

Months of preparation go into making the most of the 24 hours during which we're all feverishly pitching in somewhere. My family jumps in, too. For us it's a great chance not only to be with Marriott associates but also to soak up the positive energy and camaraderie.

Throughout the year our properties work with a huge array of nonprofits to channel surplus food, toiletries and equipment to people and organizations in need. We team up with well-known national groups plus hundreds of smaller local organizations. Our associates also put in thousands of volunteer hours on their own time, serving on various boards, building homes, coaching sports teams, tutoring, delivering hot meals, visiting sick children, mentoring and more.

———

One of the most important ways to serve our world is to be good stewards of our planet. Marriott has made huge strides in the past couple of decades in reducing our environmental footprint. Among other things, we're "greening" our $10 billion supply chain. Another goal is to reduce our energy and water consumption per room by 20 percent by 2020. And we're expanding the number of hotels certified LEED® (Leadership in Energy and Environmental Design) by the U.S. Green Building Council.

Under the umbrella of our Spirit to Preserve® program, Marriott is involved in several innovative efforts to protect the world's environment and simultaneously promote sustainable businesses and practices. In Brazil, we signed an agreement in April 2008 with the Brazilian State of Amazonas to support the first initiative of its kind to help protect 1.4 million acres of endangered rainforest. Our partnership with the government is a pioneering public/private effort to reduce greenhouse gas emissions from deforestation. The Amazon is often referred to as the "lungs of the planet," and we need to protect forests to offset development.

In Sichuan Province, China, we're collaborating with Conservation International® to support freshwater conservation. Sichuan Province is home to the largest freshwater source in the world. Launched in 2010, the Nobility of Nature project provides seed money for training and community development for villages in the area to help residents launch sustainable businesses, like making honey, that won't stress the environment.

Providing education and work opportunities to people with disabilities is a cause particularly near and dear to my family. In 1989, the Marriott Foundation for People with Disabilities® launched the Bridges From School to Work® program, to help young adults (age 17 to 22) who face mental, physical and cognitive challenges to acquire skills to enter the workplace. We support participants with program training, career planning and other skills they'll need and then match them with employers in need of entry-level talent.

So far, Bridges has placed more than 13,500 young adults with more than 3,500 employers in the United States. We have programs in Los Angeles; San Francisco; Oakland; Dallas; Chicago; Philadelphia; Washington, D.C.; Montgomery County, Md.; and Atlanta. Whenever I pop into one of our properties and meet a Bridges graduate on the job, my heart fills with joy.

Education is an area that our family's foundation has embraced for years. My parents always placed a high value on education and travel and passed those priorities along to my brother, Dick, and me. Over the years the J. Willard and Alice S. Marriott Foundation® has contributed to our family alma maters Brigham Young University and the University of Utah, plus many other universities including Cornell, San Diego State and Purdue. We know that education is one of the most important doors to opportunity.

———————

I love the fact that we can share our community volunteer ideas and experiences online now. Videos of associate and property events can be captured on smart phones and uploaded in seconds to YouTube. Stories and photos can be posted on the company's intranet, written up as blog entries (including on my blog, *Marriott on the Move*) and shared on Facebook, Twitter and other social media. People can respond, take inspiration, ask questions, offer their own tweaks. Ideas ricochet around the world as fast as we can film them or write them down. Before the Internet, it would have been impossible to have the same impact.

———————

12

WHY THE JOURNEY
IS THE REWARD

---

*"Travel is fatal to prejudice,
bigotry and narrow-mindedness."*

— MARK TWAIN, novelist and essayist

T uesday, September 11, 2001, opened like any normal workday. I arrived at my office at Marriott headquarters in suburban Bethesda, Md., at the usual early hour and was sitting in an executive meeting when someone interrupted to tell us that an airplane had flown into the World Trade Center in New York City.

It was just a few minutes before 9 a.m.

Those of us who were already in the area immediately headed for the boardroom across the hall from my office and turned on the television. The first images that came up showed billowing smoke and a gaping fiery hole in one of the two Trade Center towers. *What in the world was going on?* Like millions of other viewers, we stood transfixed by the surreal image, tried to catch the harried comments of news anchors ... and watched the second plane fly straight into the other tower at 9:03 a.m.

My mind went straight to our guests and associates in the 22-story Marriott hotel at 3 World Trade Center, sandwiched between the two 110-floor towers. Did the hotel team know what was going on? Were they already evacuating? Had anybody been hurt? The hotel's associates were well trained for emergencies, but this emergency was like nothing we'd ever seen before.

We tried frantically to get through to the hotel staff by telephone from the boardroom, to no avail. We had better luck finding out what was happening at the Marriott Financial Center on West Street, two blocks from the World Trade Center. Staff there had been able to evacuate the hundreds of guests and associates who were in the hotel at the time of the attacks.

Word soon reached us that yet another airliner had crashed into the Pentagon, just a few miles from our headquarters. Unaware of what was happening, our then CFO Arne Sorenson was driving to headquarters from a breakfast meeting in downtown Washington, D.C., when he spotted a cloud of smoke south of the city as he crossed the Potomac River on Key Bridge. The plane had just hit.

As soon as he reached headquarters, Arne joined everyone else in the boardroom, which quickly turned into command control. We were able to ascertain pretty quickly that our five hotels near the Pentagon (including one right across the street) had suffered no damage. In fact, the properties threw open their doors to take in evacuees from the damaged building. The lobby of our Residence Inn Arlington Pentagon City became an ad hoc triage center for Pentagon victims with minor injuries.

We wouldn't find out until hours later, but the story playing out at our World Trade Center hotel was a nightmare. When the first plane hit, a piece of the landing gear broke through our hotel's roof and landed in an office next to the pool. The damage set off alarms throughout the building. Marriott associates hurried from everywhere to get their emergency instructions from associate Richard Fetter in the lobby before fanning out to evacuate guests. Rich tried to print out the most current guest registry, but the hotel's computers had shut down. He nabbed an earlier printout plus emergency phone numbers.

Suddenly, the hotel lobby was awash in people — our guests, plus people fleeing from the north tower of the Trade Center. The two buildings were adjacent, connected by a door on the hotel's north side. Under the circumstances, the best exit route out of the hotel was through the Tall Ships Bar and Grill at the south end of the lobby. There, a door opened out onto Liberty Street. Everyone streamed in that direction, forming a long queue. Associate Joe Keller stationed himself at a bellhop station so he could steer people toward the exit. A police officer stationed just outside the door kept an eye on the sky and occasionally stopped people from stepping out into the path of dangerous debris tumbling from the damaged tower above.

Because our hotel was sandwiched between the World Trade Center towers, several of the fire companies that rushed to the scene poured into our lobby. Deputy Chief Thomas Galvin later recalled in a *New York Times* article that when he realized how many firemen were on hand, he sent some of them to the upper floors of the hotel to help clear guests.

In under an hour, the great majority of people who were in the hotel and lobby area had been evacuated. At 9:59 a.m. — just after Marriott associates Rich Fetter and Joe Keller had exchanged a few words about how well the evacuation was going — the south tower collapsed and split the hotel in two from top to bottom. The impact registered 2.1 on the Richter scale.

"It was like they severed the building with scissors,'" recalled firefighter Patrick Carey when he was interviewed for a *New York Times* piece about the hotel's fate on 9/11. "If you were on one side of the line you were OK. If you were on the other, you were lost."

By the time the south tower fell, the guests had evacuated and the lobby was occupied mainly by our associates, police officers and firefighters. Reinforced beams installed in the hotel following the 1993 bomb attack on the World Trade Center shielded a portion of the lobby from bearing the brunt of the impact. Rich Fetter was fortunate to be standing in a protected spot when the tower fell.

"Nicks, scrapes, little bruised here and there, but no bones broken," Rich recalled later in an interview for the *Times*.

The same could not be said of Joseph Keller, our 31-year-old director of services. One moment, he had been standing near Rich; the next moment, he was gone. Rich grabbed a radio and managed to make contact with Joe. The director of services had taken refuge on a ledge. From his precarious perch, he could see down into the bowels of the building. Joe wasn't alone. Two injured firefighters were near him, he told Rich, but not reachable from where he was.

Rescue workers began to dig through a wall of debris to reach Joe but couldn't get to him before the north tower began to collapse. The second building fell at 10:28 a.m. and shook the ground with a magnitude of 2.3. Rich Fetter was in the path of a fast-moving tidal wave of debris. A firefighter squatting behind a column grabbed him as he slid by and yanked him to safety.

With the collapse of the north tower, Joe Keller vanished. I learned later that Rose Keller, his wife, had called her husband earlier and urged him to leave. "He told me that he was evacuating the people, and I, selfishly, said, you get out," she told the *Times*. "He said, 'I'll leave here when I can.'"

When an accounting was later taken, it appeared that at least 41 firefighters who had been trying to clear the hotel were also lost. Missing, too, was Marriott associate Abdu Malahi, one of our audiovisual engineers. Abdu was last spotted on the upper floors of the hotel knocking on guest room doors during the evacuation. Within hours, the families of the two men were notified. I was deeply saddened by the loss of these Marriott associates who, like their many colleagues that day, exhibited such bravery and dedication in the face of horrific tragedy.

Eleven of the 940 registered guests at the 3 World Trade Center hotel were unaccounted for. Our guests were resettled at seven other Marriott hotels: the New York Marriott Marquis, the New York Marriott East Side, the Rihga Royal New York, the New York Marriott at the Brooklyn Bridge, the Courtyard New York Manhattan/Midtown East, the Courtyard Times Square South and the Courtyard Jersey City Newport.

For security reasons, traffic in and out of New York City was shut down. We didn't know how long our supply network might be cut off. Hotels made do with whatever food and other items they had in stock. Services were limited, but we did everything we could to watch after our guests and associates while we waited for the city to start functioning again. As the dust settled, we set up a toll-free assistance line for friends and family members who wanted to check on guests or associates. We created a human resources center at the New York Marriott East Side to answer associates' questions about pay and benefits and to provide counseling to those who wanted it. The J. Willard and Alice S. Marriott Foundation later issued a $1 million grant to establish the Marriott Associate Assistance Fund for 9/11.

Meanwhile, in Bethesda, Md., while we were still all gathered in the company's boardroom, Ed Ryan, who is now our general counsel, had leaned over to Arne Sorenson and commented, "This is going to have a huge impact on the travel industry."

Ed's assessment was spot-on. Images of the airplanes striking the two towers would play like an endless loop in the imaginations of millions of travelers for months and years to come. Hotel reservations plummeted anywhere from 30 percent to 80 percent almost immediately. Air travel slowed to a trickle. When the stock market reopened for trading on September 18, our share price fell 20 percent by day's end.

None of the reaction was surprising. Fear is a powerful force. Even with the tightening of airport security in the days following the attacks — and sometimes because of it — people became reluctant to travel.

Marriott had to adjust quickly. Plans in mid-2001 had called for the opening of 175,000 rooms over a five-year period from 1999 to 2003. At the end of second quarter 2001, 95 percent of the planned rooms were opened or under development. In the months after the attacks, we announced plans to cancel or postpone construction of more than 5,000 rooms. We kept as many people on payrolls as we could, cutting back on hours if we had to, but keeping their health benefits untouched. We also checked with our banks to be sure we could maintain enough liquidity to get us through the worst of the crisis.

I was worried about our company in the short term but even more worried about the long-term impact of the attacks on the travel industry as a whole. In the United States, one job in seven is related in some way to travel and tourism. That's no small thing. According to the World Travel & Tourism Council®, travel and tourism directly sustain more jobs than the financial services, communications and mining industries combined — not just in the United States but also in every region of the world.

Our peers in the travel industry were as troubled as I was by the likely global economic impact of the attacks. We wasted no time rallying the industry to raise awareness in the government and among the public that staying home was not the answer to 9/11 or any other terrorist events.

On September 21, 2001, just ten days after the attacks, Starwood, Marriott and others began pushing for the reopening of Reagan National Airport in Washington, D.C., as soon as possible. The hospitality industry in the Washington area alone generates $10 billion annually in revenues. We estimated that as much as $1 billion of that could simply disappear unless efforts were made to get traffic flowing again and remind the public that the nation's capital was safe and open for business.

Five days later, several major travel company CEOs and I met with Secretary of Commerce Donald Evans. In mid-October, I testified before the Senate's subcommittee on tourism. In the more than ten years since, there have been countless follow-up meetings with government officials. And many more to come, I'm sure.

As monumental as September 11 was in altering American ideas about safety and security, it wasn't the first or last time that our company has had to deal with terrorists bent on wreaking havoc. Our hotels in Islamabad, Pakistan, and in Jakarta, Indonesia, have been the sites of bombs and explosions that have taken lives and made international headlines.

Jakarta has been hit twice. In August 2003, when a car bomb went off in front of our JW Marriott Hotel in Jakarta, our response protocol was immediately activated. Ed Fuller, who was running our international operations at the time, rallied executives in Bethesda, Md., with a 2:30 a.m. phone call with the news. By 4 a.m., we had a toll-free number in place for anyone who wanted to trace guests and hotel associates. An on-site crisis center was in place hours later. Marriott associates from elsewhere in the company divided up the names of the estimated 230 guests at the hotel and the 642 staff members and spent the day calling each to be sure everyone was all right. The following day, Ed and a team of executives boarded a plane for Jakarta to provide support and follow-up.

Some companies have become skittish about international expansion, but we've stood firm with our plans to grow. Backing away for any reasons short of dire economic circumstances or ongoing security risk would be caving in to fear, in my view. At the same time, it would be naive and irresponsible not to be prepared. We and our peers in the hotel industry have redoubled security procedures at many properties. Of course, we all do our utmost to make them as unobtrusive as we can to our guests.

Mother Nature has also thrown a few curveballs our way. We've navigated through tsunamis in Thailand and Hurricane Katrina in New Orleans. The SARS (severe acute respiratory syndrome) epidemic in 2003 kept travelers away from many Asian destinations. In 2005, we coped with global worries about the deadly H5N1 "bird flu" virus. Three years later it was the H1N1 flu strain.

Lest this chapter sound as if it's all about doom and gloom, let me make clear that my main point is precisely the opposite. As the world grows smaller, thanks to innovations in travel and communications, it also promises more adventures. And more opportunities to explore, learn and grow.

Globalization is about opportunity and mobility — both geographic and economic. 3 billion people — half the world's population — entered the global economy in the past 15 years, thanks to the fall of the Berlin Wall and an explosion of economic growth across Asia, the Middle East and Latin America. At least a quarter of that three billion is poised to travel for the first time. The world is truly on the cusp of a new Golden Age of Travel.

The potential impact of so many globe trotters on the travel industry will be phenomenal. But even more critical is the impact those travelers will have on each other. Our research shows that opinion leaders and global travelers in China, India, Europe and the Americas all believe firmly that international travel is more important and more valuable than the Internet, television, movies or political diplomacy at breaking down cultural barriers and fostering peace and understanding. I agree.

That is why we need to encourage people to move around the planet — get out, explore, meet other people from other cultures.

Back when Marriott first started to build hotels overseas, our goal was focused on making Americans feel comfortable outside our country's borders. That's because Americans constituted a huge new wave of world travelers after World War II, thanks to the postwar economic boom in the United States. Our first hotel built outside the United States was in Mexico in 1969. The first Marriott located in Europe was built in Amsterdam. The first in the Middle East was the Riyadh Marriott Hotel in Saudi Arabia in 1980. In Africa, our first hotel was the Cairo Marriott in 1981. In Asia, it was Hong Kong in 1989. All had the American traveler foremost in mind.

Marriott's focus has shifted in the past 20 years as we've watched trends in international travel change. We no longer build primarily for an American audience; now we build for everyone. With so many people ready to explore beyond their borders, we're focused on our international development pipeline. Right now, Marriott hotels constitute just three percent of the world market. The potential for growth is huge. In hot markets like Brazil, Russia, India and China we're growing at a double-digit compound annual growth rate and tripling the development pipeline in those markets.

As excited as we are about the future of the global travel industry as a whole, I'm worried about the United States. The events of September 11 made officials skittish about security for the last decade. Our nation's share of the growing global travel market decreased between 2001 and 2011.

One hang-up is that we haven't promoted our own country. All the major countries have dynamic marketing efforts to get people to visit their countries. Launched a decade ago, India's colorful "Incredible India" marketing campaign is one of the best I've ever seen. In March 2012, Singapore unveiled its "Singapore — The Holiday You Take Home With You" marketing program. The United States has never had a similar national advertising program targeted at international audiences. The government would never spend the money for it.

The U.S. travel industry has been busy educating our officials about the impact of travel on economic development, job growth and tax revenues. With the U.S. economy still struggling to get traction, pumping some dollars into beefing up our tourism programs makes good economic sense. We're making some progress. In March 2010, Congress passed and President Obama signed the Travel Promotion Act of 2009 — a great step in the right direction. This law paved the way for the creation of Brand USA, a public-private partnership that is developing our nation's first coordinated marketing program overseas. In 2012, President Obama officially unveiled the program, proclaiming "America is now open for business."

The travel industry is also working hard to help Washington grasp that travel means jobs. One American job is created for every 35 people who visit the United States. But to get those international visitors, we need to make it easier and faster to get a visa, offer visa waivers for more countries and provide a welcoming experience at our borders.

The World Travel & Tourism Council predicts that travel and tourism around the world is going to grow 6 percent a year for the foreseeable future. But my bet is that travel and tourism coming out of the emerging markets of India, China and Brazil is going to be way more than that.

While we have hotels all over the world, our challenge here in the United States is, how do we get those travelers to come to America and spend their money here rather than go to Paris and elsewhere? Increased travel and tourism represents a tremendous opportunity to add hundreds of thousands of jobs and really help the U.S. economy.

To do that we have to temper the unfriendly message that the United States projected after 9/11: that foreigners really are not welcome. That's not who we are; we're a nation of immigrants, after all. Travel is in our national DNA. Security is important, but not at the cost of losing who we are at heart.

Among other things, we need to revamp our visa process to make it easier for people to choose to visit the United States rather than go somewhere else. The U.S. Commerce Department is projecting that as many as 2.5 million Brazilian travelers will be choosing world destinations in the next five years. The number of Chinese coming to this country in 2030 could be 10 to 15 million people. In 2011 alone, mainland Chinese travelers made 78 million trips overseas. They flocked to France, Australia and Singapore, but only 1 million came to the United States. That's why the United States needs to do even more to put out the welcome mat at our airports and borders.

Part of the trick is to give visitors to the United States the kind of gracious welcome that we Americans love to receive when we head to an unfamiliar place. Think how nice it is to hear a few words of greeting in your own language, see a familiar item or two on the menu, or be able to click on the television in your hotel room and catch up on your favorite sports teams. As much as people love to experience local flavor and culture when they travel, they also appreciate small touches that show that their host wants them to feel at home.

Marriott, for example, has a special welcome program for our Chinese guests called "Li Yu," which means "Serve with Courtesy" in Mandarin. Reservation confirmation letters or emails are sent to guests in Chinese. When guests arrive, they're greeted by a Mandarin-speaking associate. Chinese newspapers and television programs are available, as are tea, popular Chinese condiments and favorite foods. Another touch is the assignment of rooms and floors that include the numbers 6 and 8 — numbers that in Chinese culture are considered auspicious.

Travel can be such a potent force for good in the world. When we travel, wherever we travel, we become our own best goodwill ambassadors for world peace and understanding. With every friendly exchange, travelers triumph over the forces of fear and ignorance that lead to wars or allow terrorism to take root.

Do we really want to waste such an incredible opportunity? I hope the answer is — and will always be — no.

Metal detectors and bomb-scanning machines aren't going away. Biometrics, fingerprints and bar codes for passports are the wave of the future. But it's the human factor that counts the most.

I would love to see each of us embrace the wisdom of those who have come before us — people and cultures who recognized the power of travel to educate, to fulfill, to change the world and to change ourselves for the better with every step we take.

Who lives sees much. Who travels sees more.

— ARAB PROVERB

AFTERWORD

Whenever I gaze at one of the classic black-and-white photos of the small root beer stand that my young parents opened in 1927, and then look at all the gorgeous hotels that Marriott has built around the world, I am quite simply blown away. Our company has come such a long way from where we started.

I have, too. My first official job on the payroll at Marriott was in the accounting department when I was 14 years old. It was a summer gig. I spent my days stapling red, blue and yellow invoices together and making sure the numbers added up. That was about all I could do at that age. Knowing my dad, he probably checked my arithmetic. Twice.

Not many people know this, but my first *unofficial* association with the company goes back almost a decade earlier, to when I was about 5 years old. One day I climbed into the attic of our house and found a box of A&W Root Beer cards. I must have been old enough to read because I knew what "Free Root Beer" meant. You would take the ticket to a Hot Shoppes and hand it in; in return, you got a free soda.

The wheels started turning in my head. "I can make some money on this," I thought. So I found a paper bag, filled it with the A&W coupons and went door to door in the neighborhood. I offered them at two for a nickel. I didn't get many takers, but that was OK. I had a lot of fun trying.

I didn't know it at the time, but that short-lived entrepreneurial adventure was the first step on my life's long and happy journey with Marriott. As I step away from the CEO position that I've occupied for four decades, I can say with all candor — and without reservations — that it has been an amazing trip. I was very lucky. I found what I wanted to do early in life. That's the key to happiness. And to success, too. Because unless you are genuinely excited about going to work each day, you'll just be filling the hours. It won't be fun. And if it's not fun, you'll have a hard time achieving the success you deserve.

My dad is the one who underscored the importance of having fun on the job. He considered it so vital that he included it in a short list of guideposts he handed down to me almost 50 years ago: "Think objectively, keep a sense of humor — make the business fun for you and others," he advised.

The guideposts were tucked into a letter that he left in my desk drawer the night before he made me president of the company in 1964. He did this long before Ronald Reagan started the tradition of leaving a note behind in the oval office for the next president of the United States. I was only 32 years old when my father entrusted me with the job. He had spent 37 years building the business, establishing our reputation for excellence. The idea of following in his footsteps was daunting.

The older I get, the more I treasure that letter. My father was not one to lavish praise, but in it he told me how proud he was of me and how much confidence he had in my ability to manage the company. His words still mean so much to me that I'd like to share the letter with you.

January 20, 1964

Dear Bill:

I am mighty proud of you. Years of
preparation, work, and study have shown results.

A leader should have character, be an
example in all things. This is his greatest influence.
In this you are admirable. You have not taken
advantage of your position as my son. You remain
humble.

You have proved you can manage people
and get them to work for you. You have made a
profit--your thinker works. You are developing more
patience and understanding with people--more maturity.

It is not often a father has a son who can
step into his shoes and wear them on the basis of his
own accomplishments and ability. Being the operating
manager of a business on which probably 30,000
people depend for a livelihood is a frightening
responsibility, but I have the greatest confidence
you will build a team that will insure the continued
success of a business that has been born through
years of toil and devotion by many wonderful people.
I have written down a few guideposts--all born out
of my experience and ones I wish I could have followed
more closely.

Love and best wishes.

Sincerely,

J. Willard Marriott

Mr. J. Willard Marriott, Jr.

Letter from my dad to me when I became president of Hot Shoppes in 1964.

I hope I lived up to his expectations and will leave behind a legacy that would make him proud of what Marriott has accomplished in its 85 years.

———

As I look ahead, the next phase of my life promises to be a little quieter, a bit less hectic, but still filled with fun. I'll be able to spend more time with my family, enjoy our lake home in New Hampshire and relax on family vacations at two of my favorite destinations: the Camelback Inn near Scottsdale, Ariz., and our Harbor Beach Marriott Resort & Spa in South Florida. I will continue to visit our hotels, as I always have. That's one of the best perks of my job, and I don't plan to give it up any time soon. I'll now have more time, too, to champion the tourism and travel industries, here in the United States and around the world.

As executive chairman of Marriott, I'll continue to be involved in ways large and small with the company, but others will now have their turn at leading us into the future. And what a future it's going to be. I'm thrilled to be going along for the ride, knowing that our company is in the very best of hands. It promises to be an unforgettable trip, and I intend to savor every moment. As one centuries-old Chinese proverb wisely observes: *The journey is the reward.*

———

To Bill:

1. Keep physically fit, mentally and spiritually strong.

2. Guard your habits - bad ones will destroy you.

3. Pray about every difficult problem.

4. Study and follow professional management principles. Apply them logically and practically to your organization.

5. People are No. 1 - their development, loyalty, interest, team spirit. Develop managers in every area. This is your prime responsibility.

6. Decisions - men grow making decisions and assuming responsibility for them.

    a. Make crystal clear what their decisions are - and what decisions you make.

    b. Have all the facts and counsel - then decide and stick to it.

7. Criticism - Don't criticise people but appraise them with their supervisor only (or someone assigned to do this). Remember, anything you say about someone may (and usually) gets back.

8. See the good in people and try to develop them.

9. Inefficiency - If it cannot be overcome and employee is obviously incapable of the job, find a job he can do or terminate now.

10. Manage your time:
    Short conversations - to the point.
    Make every minute on the job count.
    Work fewer hours - some of us waste half our time.

11. Delegate and hold accountable for results.

12. Details:
      Let staff take care of them
      Save energy for planning, thinking, working with
         department heads, promoting new ideas (few
         have them)
      Don't do anything someone else can do *for you* -

13. Don't try to do employee's job for him - counsel and
      suggest.

14. Ideas:
      Keep a business alive
      Know what your competitors are doing and planning
         (auto companies have expensive spies)
      Encourage all management to think about better
         ways and give suggestions on anything that will
         improve business.

15. Think objectively, keep a sense of humor -
      make the business fun for you and others.

Dad
Jan. 21/64
Washington D.C.

The original articulation of the Guideposts to Management, which accompanied Dad's letter to me.

*"Don't tell me how educated you are;
tell me how much you traveled."*

— MUHAMMAD

M-A-R-R-I-O-T-T

This is my "recipe for success" that I shared at the Global General Managers meeting in Los Angeles in March 2012:

M – is for "More." More satisfied customers ... more opportunity for our people ... more financial returns to our owners, franchisees and investors ... and, of course, more hotels in more cities and countries.

A – is for "Ask." I've always tried to hire people who are smarter than I am. I ask a lot of questions and listen to their suggestions. You should, too.

R – is for "Respect." Be humble, respect others and you will have an unbeatable team!

R – The second *r* is for "Recognition." I write more than 700 notes of appreciation every year to customers and associates. I try to say "thank you" as often as possible.

I – is for "Innovation." We were the first hotel company to develop and acquire multiple brands. Innovation continues with more exciting lobbies, guest rooms and leading technology.

O – is for "Opportunity." As we've seen, the driving force behind our core values is to open doors to opportunity for all.

T – is for the "Tenacity" I learned from my parents. As my dad said, "Success is never final."

T – And the final "*t*" is for "Time." Don't waste it — make every minute count!

MARRIOTT MILESTONES

1927 Hugh Colton and J. Willard Marriott pool $3,000 each to finance an A&W franchise, root beer concentrate and restaurant equipment in Washington, D.C. On May 20, the company's first root beer stand opens at 3128 14th Street NW. Hot food is added later, and the name The Hot Shoppe is adopted. Marriott marries Alice Sheets on June 9, and the couple settles in the nation's capital permanently.

1928 Hugh Colton sells his shares back to the Marriotts for $5,000 and moves back to Utah.

1929 Hot Shoppes Inc. is officially incorporated in the state of Delaware.

1932 J. Willard (Bill) Marriott, Jr., is born in Washington, D.C. The company opens a Hot Shoppe in Baltimore, Md. — its first restaurant outside of Washington, D.C.

1937 Hot Shoppes pioneers airline catering at Hoover Field (current site of the Pentagon) in Washington, D.C., selling boxed lunches to passengers. In-Flite catering division begins service to Eastern Air Lines and American Airlines.

1939 Richard (Dick) Marriott, younger brother of Bill, is born in Washington, D.C. Hot Shoppes launches its food service management business with an account at the U.S. Treasury building.

1941-45 During World War II, Hot Shoppes feeds many of the thousands of workers who move to the nation's capital to work in defense plants and government complexes.

1946 Bill Marriott begins his first job with Hot Shoppes at age 14. His assignment: stapling invoices together for the accounting department. During his high school years, he works in the D.C.-area Hot Shoppes cooking burgers, washing dishes and mopping floors.

1946-1947 Hot Shoppes expands its postwar industrial customer base by operating cafeterias at the General Motors plant in Georgia and the Ford Motor Company plant in Virginia.

1953 Hot Shoppes Inc. stock first offered to public at $10.25 per share. Offering sells out in two hours.

1954 Bill Marriott graduates from the University of Utah with a degree in banking and finance, followed by a two-year stint (1954–56) as a ship's supply officer aboard the *USS Randolph*. While in the Navy, he proposes — long distance — to Donna Garff, daughter of a professor at the University of Utah. Total annual sales for the company in 1954 reach $21.5 million.

1955 The company launches what will become the highway food service division with two snack bars on the New York State Thruway and begins serving food at Children's Hospital in Washington, D.C., its first hospital account, and at American University, its first education account. Corporate headquarters are consolidated at 5161 River Road, Washington, D.C. The site includes 11 acres, a test kitchen, a modern employee cafeteria and a print shop.

1956 Bill Marriott joins the company full-time. Sales exceed $29 million.

1957 Twin Bridges, "The World's Largest Motor Hotel Owned and Operated by Hot Shoppes Inc." opens in Arlington, Va. The 365 air-conditioned rooms also feature telephones, radios and televisions; a Hot Shoppe restaurant; a barber shop; a variety store;

a gasoline station; a swimming pool; and adjacent guest parking. A drive-in registration desk "enables guests to register in their automobiles. Bicycle attendants will guide guests to their rooms." Bill Marriott takes over management of the company's new lodging division. Company opens its first *Mighty Mo* curb-service restaurant. Total annual sales for the year exceed $36 million.

1958 The Hot Shoppes' second hotel — Key Bridge Marriott — is under construction. According to the company's annual report for 1958, the facility will have 210 rooms and is "ideally situated to accommodate tourists and businessmen visiting the city of Washington."

1959 Key Bridge Marriott opens. Two-year-old Debbie Marriott, Bill and Donna's daughter, snips the ribbon. Bill Marriott is named vice president, hotel operations. The company's first Sirloin & Saddle specialty restaurant opens in the Twin Bridges hotel: "The room features a Western atmosphere where the rough textures of the bricks, carpets and wood paneling provide strong accents. It is interesting that the weathered oak paneling used for the walls is over 100 years old and was brought from our Fairfield Farm in the foothills of the Appalachian Mountains in Virginia." Sales have almost doubled since 1955 to $46 million.

1960 Third motor hotel — Dallas-Stemmons Marriott — opens. Marriott's hotel growth strategy focuses on targeting suburban locations near airports and major convention cities. Total sales for the year exceed $54 million. Employees: 7,000.

1961 Fourth motor hotel — Philadelphia Marriott — opens. The facility's three restaurants include the company's first venture into Polynesian food, the Kona Kai, in honor of Hawaii, which became a state two years earlier. In what will become a major financing strategy in subsequent years, three of the company's hotel properties are sold and leased back as a means of raising additional capital for growth.

1962 Main focus of company's lodging division is on adding major convention facilities, exhibit space and rooms to existing hotels. Marriott recruits veteran "hotel men" from other companies, including Hilton and Sheraton, to expand its lodging management team. The company installs its first computer, an IBM 1401.

1963 Ground is broken for company's fifth hotel — the Atlanta Marriott — the first major new convention hotel in the city since 1930. The Hot Shoppes' In-Flite catering division is "one of the largest operations in the industry, serving 25 airlines at 10 major airports." The company opens food service facilities at the Smithsonian Institution and the newly opened Dulles International Airport. Hot Shoppes reorganizes into six major operating divisions: service restaurants, cafeterias, motor hotels, airline catering, institutional food service and manufacturing.

1964 Company changes its name to Marriott–Hot Shoppes Inc. At age 32, Bill Marriott is elected president and a member of the board of directors. Company begins to receive inquiries about its willingness to manage hotels on a fee basis. Total annual sales exceed $84 million. Employees: 9,600.

1965 Fifth hotel — Atlanta Marriott — opens. Sixth and seventh Marriott hotels are in the planning stages. Marriott's first fast-food restaurant, Hot Shoppes Jr., boasting a "15-cent hamburger," opens in suburban Washington, D.C.

1966 Sixth hotel — Saddlebrook, N.J., Marriott — opens. The six Marriott hotels check in more than 1 million guests during the year. The Hot Shoppes menu includes 385 items. In-Flite goes international with a flight kitchen in Caracas, Venezuela. Sales reach $123 million, a 25 percent increase over the previous year.

1967 In November of its 40th anniversary year, Marriott–Hot Shoppes Inc. renames itself Marriott Corporation. Company purchases the 22-unit Big Boy coffee shop chain from founder Bob Wian. Company acquires its first resort, the Camelback Inn® in Scottsdale, Ariz. Ground is broken for largest flight kitchen ever built, at JFK International Airport in New York. Hotel construction is under way in Boston and Houston. Expansions planned at Philadelphia, Key Bridge and Atlanta Marriott hotels.

1968 Marriott acquires Robee's fast-food chain and develops Roy Rogers brand name. First Roy Rogers restaurant opens in Fairfax, Va. Marriott Inn franchising program announced. Marriott is listed on New York Stock Exchange for the first time. Approximately 90 percent of company's sales come from food and beverage sales, and 10 percent from lodging.

1969 Marriott enters international lodging market with a leased hotel (Paraiso) in Acapulco, Mexico. Company purchases major New York City hotel — Essex House. Eleven Marriott hotels are now open. Company's architecture and construction division assures Marriott maintains control over design quality. Total annual sales for the year exceed $257 million, $58 million of which comes from the lodging division. Marriott consolidates into three divisions: restaurant operations, In-Flite and hotels.

1970 Sales for the year total $315 million. First franchised Marriott Inns open, mostly in Midwest cities. Twelve-story tower added to Key Bridge hotel. Marriott World Travel is established. Operating units: 382. Employees: more than 26,000.

1971 Marriott's first Joshua Tree restaurant opens in McLean, Va. Hot Shoppes Jr. — Marriott's entry into fast food — is struggling against proliferation of *McDonald's* and other chains. Some Hot Shoppes Jr. locations will be converted to Roy Rogers units. Diversification push begins. First of a series of recession-plagued years. The annual report notes: "Marriott Hotels felt the sting of the sluggish economy most severely, and were unable to contribute as much to our profit growth as we had hoped."

In December, Marriott enters Sun Line cruise ship partnership and announces plans for Great America theme parks. Fiscal year 1971 sales: $347 million.

1972   Marriott acquires Farrell's Ice Cream Parlour chain. The company now has 18 hotels, 12 of which have been built in the past six years. Bill Marriott is named chief executive officer of Marriott Corporation. Total annual sales for fiscal year 1972 exceed $422 million, a 20 percent increase over previous year. Marriott's stock splits for the fourth time, two-for-one; earlier splits came in 1960, 1965 and 1968.

1973   First lodging management contracts are negotiated, marking the beginning of Marriott's evolution into a hotel management company. Company also acquires security business, the Hallmark Corporation, and renames it Marriott Security Systems. Restaurant division launches more specialty lines: Phineas Prime Rib and Franklin Stove. Marriott acquires Sam Lord's Castle, a well-known resort property in Barbados. Sun Line's third cruise ship, the *Stella Solaris*, makes her maiden voyage. Total annual sales exceed $500 million.

1974   Economic recession of early 1970s continues, curtailing leisure and business travel. Company nonetheless adds 118 units, bringing the total to 688 as of midyear, doubling Marriott's restaurants, food service accounts and In-Flite kitchens in just five years. Company serves 600,000 people each day in its restaurants, hotels, airline flights and cruise ships. Construction is underway for Great America theme parks in Santa Clara, Calif., and Gurnee, Ill.

1975   The Cypriot War disrupts the first full season of Marriott's partnership in Sun Line cruise ships. The company opens seven new hotels and 52 new restaurants, acquires a dozen more restaurants, but cancels six hotel projects and takes a $500 million write-off of development expenses due to recession. Marriott's first European hotel opens in Amsterdam. Marriott experiences its first earnings decline in 15 years, thanks in part to recession, inflation and Sun Line's losses.

1976 Marriott's two Great America parks open during Bicentennial year. Marriott Security Systems division is sold after only three years. Total sales exceed $890 million, a 21.6 percent increase over previous year. Marriott's In-Flite division is the largest independent caterer to airlines, serving 120 U.S. and foreign carriers.

1977 Sales hit $1 billion during Marriott's 50th anniversary year. The company's financial philosophy changes, launching an era of debt financing that will fuel growth in the 1980s. Among other things, plans are underway to sell several of the company's existing hotels and take back management contracts. Annual report announces that "soon, more than 50 percent of our hotel rooms are expected to be under management agreement." Company breaks ground for new corporate headquarters in Bethesda, Md.

1978 First Middle Eastern Marriott, Khurais Marriott, opens in Riyadh, Saudi Arabia. As part of its strategy to move away from hotel ownership to hotel management, Marriott has already sold more than half its room capacity to investors. Announces 20/20 financial goals: 20 percent return on equity, 20 percent growth in sales. Architecture and Construction (A&C) division completes $100 million in construction in a single year. Marriott hotels are now operating in 45 cities.

1979 The company sells Marriott World Travel and company's dinner house division to focus on growing the lodging division. Total annual sales increase by $500 million in just two years to $1.5 billion. By the end of 1979, 50 hotels are in various stages of construction. Marriott begins repurchases of stock and sells off $90 million in "idle or marginally profitable assets."

1980 About 70 percent of all Marriott guest rooms are now owned by investors. Hotels begin to dominate company's overall sales, accounting for more than half. Nearly 100 hotels are in the A&C pipeline, twice the projection made in 1979. In a major tender offer, the company buys back nearly one-fourth of its outstanding common stock.

1981 One hundredth hotel opens — Maui Marriott Resort, Hawaii. Marriott's annual sales surpass $2 billion, doubling in less than five years. Company arranges first limited partnership to finance 11 hotels by a syndicate of commercial banks. Planning begins on Courtyard by Marriott®, the company's first entry into the moderate-priced lodging market. The lodging division sees a 40 percent increase in rooms in one year — the system now has 40,000 rooms in 74 cities. The annual report notes that Marriott is one of the "world's largest real estate developers, creating about $1 billion of product annually." Marriott's restaurant division continues streamlining and narrows its focus to expanding Roy Rogers fast food restaurants and Big Boy coffee shops.

1982 Marriott estimates that its employees handle 6 million customer contacts each day. Gino's fast-food chain is acquired for conversion into Roy Rogers units. In-Flite division receives big boost with acquisition of Host International, an 85-year-old food service company with a specialty in airport concession operations. Marriott sells Farrell's Ice Cream Parlour chain. The lodging division reaches $1 billion in annual sales for the first time. An average of one Marriott hotel opens every two weeks. Lodging expansion plans "will enable Marriott to become the world's largest manager — as distinct from franchiser — of hotels."

1983 First two Courtyard by Marriott® hotels open outside of Atlanta, Ga., surprising the moderate-priced lodging market. The company now has approximately 55,000 guest rooms in 133 hotels in 79 cities in the United States and internationally. Halo hotel properties are acquired in Paris (Prince de Galles in

1983) and London (London Marriott in 1984). Ground is broken for two Marriott Marquis® hotels designed by John Portman. Employees: over 109,000.

1984 Company's flagship, the JW Marriott® Hotel, opens in Washington, D.C. Company acquires American Resorts Group. Restaurant division continues to streamline by putting its Mexican restaurants and more dinner houses up for sale. Marriott agrees to sell Essex House to Japanese investors, an early sign of fast-growing Japanese interest in American real estate. Marriott Honored Guest Awards frequent-stay program is established to build brand loyalty. Marriott bows out of the theme park business with the sale of both of its Great America theme parks. Total annual sales reach $3.5 billion. Marriott's sales and profits have doubled since 1980 and increased tenfold since 1971. Lodging now accounts for nearly half of the company's total sales. Marriott's hotels receive more Mobil Four- and Five-Star and AAA Four- and Five-Diamond awards than any other lodging chain.

1985 New York Marriott Marquis® opens. Marriott acquires food service giants Gladieux Corporation and Service Systems Corporation. Company also acquires the Howard Johnson concern; under the deal, the hotels are sold to Prime Motor Inn and restaurants are kept for conversion into Big Boys. In what will prove to be an overly optimistic projection, Marriott announces that it should reach $10 billion in annual sales by the early 1990s. (Goal is eventually reached in 1996.) J. Willard Marriott dies at age 84. One month later, Bill Marriott is elected chairman of the board.

1986 Marriott acquires Saga Corporation, a major institutional food service and restaurant company. In-Flite kitchens serve more than 150 airlines. Marriott's Orlando World Center — a 1,500-room convention facility — opens. Company's stock splits five-for-one. Marriott is rated the number-one hotel company by *Business Travel News*.

1987 Marriott now has 100,000 guest rooms, more than triple the number in 1980. Company acquires extended-stay Residence Inn® chain and opens first Fairfield Inn® properties (an economy "rooms-only" product) and Marriott Suites®. Lodging system now includes 361 properties. Marriott sells Big Boy franchise rights. The company exits Sun Line cruise ships after 15 years. Company's contract food services division contributes $2.9 billion, lodging $2.6 billion and restaurants $879 million to the company's annual sales. Company serves nearly eight million meals each day.

1988 The majority of Marriott's 451 hotels are now in the limited-service segment, a major philosophical change for a company that has been identified primarily with full-service lodging for most of its existence. Marriott itself owns only one out of every 10 rooms under the Marriott flag. A&C division develops $1.4 billion of hotels this year. Backlog of unsold hotels begins to build as sluggish-ness in real estate market sets in. In spite of Marriott's growing public identification with lodging, the company still owns 1,100 restaurants in 23 states. Food and beverage sales in all divisions of the company account for almost three-quarters of the company's annual revenues. Allie's restaurant, a new family restaurant concept, is launched. Company sales top $7.3 billion.

1989 Five hundredth hotel opens in Warsaw, Poland. Marriott's lodging system now includes 134,000 rooms in 539 hotels. First Marriott hotel limited partnership is sold to Japanese investors. The company's long-term debt stands at nearly $3.3 billion — a record — as the company's backlog of hotel properties and the state of the American hotel industry begin to worry Wall Street. During a major corporate restructuring, Marriott sells off its restaurant and In-Flite divisions in a historic move that cuts the company loose from its original roots. The company opens its first life-care retirement communities — the Quadrangle in Haverford, Pa., and the Fairfax in Alexandria, Va. Marriott's workforce stands at approximately 230,000. Bill Marriott suffers three heart attacks between October and December.

1990 Marriott adds 100 hotels — a rate of two new properties a week — adding 16,000 rooms to the system. Approximately 57 new properties are scheduled to open in 1991. Nikkei index loses almost 40 percent of its value between January and October, causing Japanese investors to withdraw from American real estate market. Marriott turns off hotel development pipeline as the U.S. real estate market crashes. The company's debt ratings were downgraded but remain investment quality. Hotel franchising is mentioned for the first time as a growth vehicle for the company. Marriott's Architecture & Construction department is dismantled, and more than 1,000 people are laid off. Debt level reaches $3.6 billion at year-end. Marriott institutes a salary freeze, using a graduated timetable and weighting the burden toward senior staff.

1991 Marriott emphasizes in its annual report that it does "not intend to sacrifice value" by selling its backlog of hotels "at low prices to expedite transactions." Company announces that the lodging division will focus on franchising, conversions and international markets for future growth. Leveraging of brand names ("branding") will also be a platform for expansion. Marriott offers 59 million room nights a year. Company reduces its long-term debt level from a high of $3.6 billion to $2.9 billion.

1992 Marriott announces intention to split into two companies. Host Marriott will retain company-owned hotels and most of company's long-term debt; Marriott International will become a management services company. The two companies will maintain separate boards of directors and other administrative systems. Bill Marriott is slated to be president, CEO and chairman of Marriott International. His brother, Richard Marriott, will be chairman of Host Marriott. Some bondholders react by filing lawsuits. Total annual sales reach $8.7 billion.

1993 Company split becomes official on October 5. Marriott International's lodging division reorganizes, consolidates and streamlines itself along brand lines — a natural outgrowth of the company's decade-old segmentation drive. Nonlodging management services account for just under half of Marriott International's sales. Marriott hotels total 784 in the United States and 22 other countries. Total annual sales for Marriott International are $8 billion — up from $7.7 billion — after adjusting for split.

1994 Back in growth mode once again, Marriott International outlines plans to add 100,000 guest rooms by 1999, two-thirds in limited service and one-third in full service. Franchising will be a "key driver of room growth" in the limited-service category. International lodging also becomes a special focus of the company's growth strategy.

1995 One thousandth hotel opens in Kauai, Hawaii. Marriott International acquires a 49 percent interest in The Ritz-Carlton chain, with option to purchase remaining interest. "The Room That Works" is introduced in 15 properties, providing work space and communications features for business travelers. Total annual sales for Marriott International reach almost $9 billion; $5.3 billion is contributed by lodging, and $3.6 billion is contributed by management services.

1996 Marriott International's Senior Living Services division acquires the Forum Group, which doubles Marriott's presence in this industry. Britain's Whitbread hotels become Marriott hotel franchisees. Launch of Marriott.com. After working with Marriott during the company's split, attorney Arne Sorenson joins Marriott International. Marriott International employs 192,000 people. Total annual sales for Marriott International top $10 billion.

1997 Marriott International rolls out its new Marriott Rewards® program, allowing guests to earn points to redeem at any of

Marriott's lodging brands. Marriott International acquires the Renaissance Hotel Group for $1 billion. The acquisition adds three established lodging brands (Renaissance®, Ramada International and New World) and doubles Marriott's overseas presence.

1998 As part of its long-term growth strategy, Marriott International spins off a new public company comprised of its lodging, senior living and distribution services businesses. Immediately following the spinoff, Marriott's food service and facilities management business (Marriott Management Services) merges with the North American operations of Sodexho Alliance. The merged company is renamed Sodexho Marriott Services Inc. Number of lodging properties grows to 1,500 with the opening of the Renaissance® Parc 55 Hotel in San Francisco. Completion of purchase of majority ownership in The Ritz-Carlton® opens the door to the addition of more high-end brands to Marriott International.

1999 The last Hot Shoppe closes on December 2, in Marlow Heights, Md. Marriott's Spirit To Serve Our Communities program is launched. Systemwide sales are nearly $18 billion. Expansion plans include a major focus on China.

2000 End of an era: Alice S. Marriott passes away in April. Her death marks the end of the first and founding generation of company management. Marriott International reaches its "2000 by 2000" goal when the Tampa, Fla., Marriott opens. Lawsuit by investors who sued Marriott International over the 1992 split of the company is settled.

2001 By early 2001, company has 7.5 percent domestic market share, 3 percent of the global market. Marriott and Hyatt set up Avendra, an Internet-based procurement network for the hospitality industry. Sodexho is sold. Plans as of mid-2001 call for opening 175,000 rooms across all Marriott International lodging brands over a five-year period from 1999 to 2003. At the end of second quarter 2001, 95 percent of the planned rooms have opened or are under development. During the summer, the economy slows, bringing with it a drop-off in lodging demand. The bursting of the heady dot.com bubble in mid-2000 begins to put a damper on business travel.

The 22-story New York Marriott World Trade Center hotel is destroyed and two associates lose their lives when the World Trade Center collapses following a terrorist attack on September 11, 2001. The nearby Marriott Financial Center also suffers extensive damage. The travel industry as a whole is affected by public fears of terrorism after 9/11. Hotel reservations plummet as people refuse to travel. The airline, finance and insurance industries take a beating on Wall Street on September 18, the first day of trading after 9/11. Marriott's share price falls 20 percent. Bill Marriott becomes a leading spokesman in the travel industry for getting people back in the air and on the road. His familiar name and face and his esteem in the hotel industry prove invaluable in the industry's public outreach efforts.

2002 Marriott International joins forces with Hilton Hotels, Hyatt, Six Continents Hotels and Starwood Hotels to buy an existing service called Travelweb.com to sell rooms over the Internet. Bill Marriott rings the closing bell at the New York Stock Exchange on May 20, 2002, to mark the company's 75th anniversary. The company opens its 2,500th hotel, the luxurious JW Marriott® Desert Ridge Resort & Spa, near Phoenix. Company exits Marriott Distribution Services. The company commits to one of the largest rollouts of Wi-Fi in the hotel industry — one of many moves in the next decade to meet customer demand for access to high-speed services.

2003 Company exits senior living services business. Sunrise Senior Living deal formally closes in March; the rest is sold by September 2003. U.S. military involvement in Iraq renews travel jitters that threaten the tourism industry, but Marriott stands firm on its expansion plans into the Middle East and elsewhere.

2004 Travel picks up, thanks to a strengthening economy, renewed business travel and an uptick in meetings and conferences. With an eye on the 2008 Olympics in China, Marriott International ramps up its expansion plans for Asia.

2005 Marriott forms a joint venture with Whitbread PLC to acquire Whitbread's portfolio of 46 franchised Marriott and Renaissance® hotels. In response to Westin's successful Heavenly Bed initiative, Marriott rolls out Revive®, a global bedding program, across eight brands and in more than 2,400 hotels. The massive investment is part of an overall effort by Marriott International to "reinvent" and "refresh" most of its existing properties to reflect up-to-date styles and standards. Hurricane Katrina slams into New Orleans in August, flooding three of the company's hotels and affecting eight others.

2006 Marriott purchases the largest hotel in Paris: the 782-room Paris Rive Gauche Hotel & Conference Center. Another high profile project is L.A. LIVE, a mixed-use development project that will include two hotels, luxury residences, a 7,000-seat live performance venue, a movie theatre, fine dining and much more. Marriott's role in the project includes an 876-room Marriott Hotel, a 124-room Ritz-Carlton® Hotel and approximately 216 condominium units called The Residences® at The Ritz–Carlton®. By the end of 2006, Marriott.com is one of the Internet's largest retailers.

2007 The company marks both its 80th anniversary and its 50th year in lodging. Bill Marriott launches his blog, *Marriott on the Move* in January. In June, Marriott International announces a unique partnership with hotel designer Ian Schrager to create a collection of luxury "boutique" hotels under the brand EDITION®. The partnership reflects the decision by Marriott International to update its image by building more one-of-a-kind, high-end properties.

2008 By mid-2008, it is clear that the U.S. economy is heading toward recession. Financial markets are in turmoil. The travel industry is affected by lower demand. The company continues to follow its expansion game plan but adjusts its financial expectations downward, especially on the timeshare front. In September, *BusinessWeek* names Marriott International one of the "100 Best Places to Launch a Career." In July 2008 Bill Marriott's *Marriott on the Move* blog is featured on *NBC Nightly News*. The 18-month-old blog is credited with generating $2.6 million in gross property-level sales in 2008. Bill Marriott continues his post-9/11 industry statesman role on key issues for the travel industry during the economic downturn.

2009 Arne M. Sorenson is named president and chief operating officer. Timeshare division continues to struggle even as it celebrates its 25th anniversary; contract sales in the segment decline 38 percent over the course of the year. Revenues total $10.9 billion in 2009 compared to $12.9 billion in 2008. Total fees in 2009 are $1.084 million, a decrease of 22 percent from 2008. Marriott.com undergoes a complete revamping. Marriott News Center debuts online. At the close of 2009, the company's worldwide pipeline of hotels under construction, awaiting conversion or approved for development totaled nearly 100,000 rooms at year-end.

2010 Upscale Autograph Collection® debuts in four categories: Boutique Arts, Iconic Historic, Boutique Chic and Luxury Redefined. Within a year of introduction, the Autograph Collection includes 13 properties, ranging from The Cosmopolitan™ of Las Vegas to the The Algonquin Hotel in New York City. In March, President Obama signs the Travel Promotion Act of 2009, legislation on which Bill Marriott worked hard for passage. Marriott International restructures itself into four continental divisions. As part of the company's Spirit To Serve Our Communities program, Marriott International teams with Conservation International to create the Nobility of Nature initiative to support fresh water conservation and sustainable business development in rural communities in China's Sichuan Province. By the end of the first quarter of 2010, a record 39 percent of the company's development pipeline is outside of North America, as are two-thirds of rooms under construction. First EDITION hotel opens in Waikiki, Hawaii, in October. Marriott International announces a joint venture with AC Hotels, a Spanish developer specializing in urban, four-star hotels to create AC Hotels by Marriott with focus on markets in Spain, Italy and Portugal. Marriott International announces plans to spin off the timeshare business into a separate company in 2011.

2011 EDITION opens in Istanbul, Turkey. Marriott Mobile goes global by debuting an app in five languages: English, Chinese, Spanish, German and French. In May, Marriott International increases its cash dividend by 14 percent — another positive sign of economic recovery. In October, Marriott International's board of directors formally approves the spinoff of Marriott Vacation Club International to Marriott Vacations Worldwide Corporation (MVW). MVW begins trading on November 22 under the symbol VAC. On December 13, Bill Marriott is elected executive chairman of Marriott International's board of directors after stepping down as CEO. Arne Sorenson is named president and CEO — the company's third CEO in 85 years and the first without the surname Marriott. The roles become effective March 31, 2012. Total revenues at year-end: more than $12 billion.

2012 *FORTUNE* magazine recognizes Marriott International as one of the "100 Best Companies to Work For" for the 15th consecutive year and singles it out as a "social media star." Marriott International and its brands also have a strong presence on social media. *Marriott on the Move*, Bill Marriott's blog, is now available in Mandarin. The original $1 million investment in Marriott.com now generates $7 billion in revenues annually. Marriott International and five other leading hotel companies debut RoomKey.com, a comprehensive search engine for booking rooms. In January, Marriott International is one of 32 companies named a "Top Employer in China" by the CRF Institute. Company has more than 3,800 lodging properties in 73 countries and territories. The company is recognized for the fifth time as one of the World's Most Ethical Companies by the Ethisphere Institute. Bill Marriott turns 80 and becomes executive chairman of Marriott International and Arne Sorenson formally steps into the role of the company's third chief executive officer. The company welcomes Central Park's iconic Essex House as a JW Marriott. Marriott completes acquisition of Gaylord Hotels brand and management company. Employees: more than 300,000 at managed and franchised hotels worldwide.

Venture all; see what fate brings.

— VIETNAMESE PROVERB

INDEX

"In this wonderful book, my good friend, Bill Marriott, shares valuable insight on how to succeed in business. More importantly, however, he shares valuable insight on how to succeed in life. His 'Recipe for Success' especially is a must-read."

— PRESIDENT GEORGE H. W. BUSH

"Bill Marriott is one of the best entrepreneurial minds in the business. He knows what it takes to build brands, relationships and a winning corporate culture. *Without Reservations* is a compelling story of how best-in-class service, integrity, loyalty and leadership turned a small, family business into one of the world's most respected companies."

— KEN CHENAULT, CEO and Chairman, American Express

"Valuable real-world lessons for leaders at every level from an inspirational and visionary business icon, who is a tireless advocate for the significant role travel plays in building our economy, putting people to work in rewarding long-term careers and enhancing public diplomacy."

— ROGER J. DOW, President and CEO, U.S. Travel Association

"Bill Marriott is a remarkable man who tells a remarkable story. Everyone — young and old — can learn something from his lessons on leadership. He has created a hotel company that is successful, not just because of its profits, but because of the opportunities it has created for people around the world."

— MRS. LAURA BUSH, Former First Lady of the United States

"*Without Reservations* is is a testament to how a company creates a long-term competitive advantage in a service economy — it is all about the culture. Bill Marriott is the icon of the hotel industry today because he understands this principle better than anyone I have ever met. *Without Reservations* is a great read for those not just in our industry, but across our service economy."

— MICHAEL D. JOHNSON, Dean — E.M. Statler Professor
Cornell University — School of Hotel Administration